E-Commerce Redefined

CONTENTS:

Introduction:	6
Shopify	8
What is Shopify?	8
How Does Shopify Work?	10
What Are Some Of The Pros Of Shopify?	11
What Are Some Of The Cons Of Spotify?	14
Features On All Plans	17
Features on The Shopify Plan	22
Features On The Advanced Shopify Plan	23
Features You May Not Have Heard About	24
Using Shopify For Your E-Commerce Business	27
Figuring Out What To Sell On Shopify	31
Market Research	31
Focus on The Demand	34
Check the Competition	35
Determine If Anything Is Going To Set You Apart From The Pack	36
Put Quality First	37
Digital Products	38
Physical Products	39
Subscription Products	41
Services	42
Setting up Your Shopify Store	45
Customizing Your Shopify Store	49
Expanding Your Product Line	56

FBA	60
What Is Amazon Fba?	60
Is Amazon FBA the right platform for you?	61
Why People Pay More on Amazon?	68
Amazon Selling Options	72
How Selling on Amazon Works?	76
How To Get Started	80
The Seller Central.	82
Payment Gateways	83
Products	91
Approaching suppliers	92
Edging Past Your Competition	95
Dealing with Suppliers	97
Branding and Packaging	98
Product Names	100
Listing	102
Product Title	102
Conversion Rate	103
Creating an Amazon Listing	105
Shipping	109
Freight Forwarders	110
Traction and Feedback	111
A) Traction	111
B) Feedback	114
1. Take into consideration FBA specific campaigns	115
2. Confirm That You Are Soliciting	116
3. Be Extra Careful On What You Are "Acquiring"	117
Tricks and Tactics	120

Online Business Redefined

Harnessing the Power of Shopify & FBA To Build Your Empire

Brandon Cutler

© Copyright 2018 by Brandon Cutler - All rights reserved.

1. How To Deal With Negative Reviews.   **120**
2. Free Inventory From Your House   **121**
3. Joining Amazon FBA Facebook Groups   **122**
4. Using Dunnage For Shipments   **123**
5. Free Boxes From Grocery Stores For Shipment   **123**
6. Lighter Fluid To Remove Price Stickers   **124**
7. Free Inventory From Freecycle.Org   **125**
8. Boxes From Arbitrage Purchases   **126**

Conclusion   135

Introduction:

Today, there are so many ways of generating income for yourself outside of that normal 9 to 5 desk job that so many of us are trying desperately to escape from. The sheer number of options out there is overwhelming and we find ourselves unable to be decisive and break through our mental blocks to achieve real success because we simply don't know where to begin. The dream of passive income is actually not a dream. It's a goal that you can work towards. It won't happen overnight, but with patience, perseverance and resourcefulness, you will be able to achieve that goal.

The problem for most of us, as I said, is that we don't know where to start. We might have an idea for a business or else we simply just know what type of business we want to operate, but that's about all we know. In order to achieve the success, we're looking for, we need to make use of the resources, tools, and services available to us to give us the best chance of success while also greatly reducing the risk involved.

Starting a physical product business can be extremely risky if you don't know what you're doing. Many people have lost hundreds of thousands if not millions of their own dollars and those of their investors, backers and even family and friends by investing heavily in a physical product business that never became profitable. Does this mean that physical product businesses are too risky or that you shouldn't try to start one yourself? Absolutely not. The reason I say no is because you are different than those people. You are reading this book. You're already aware of what most people aren't. There are 2 very transformative tools and platforms that will help you launch and scale your business with minimum risk with maximum opportunity for profitability and growth: Amazon FBA & Shopify. Once you're able to understand these two platforms and how to harness their power to build a viable business, you'll be fortified and ready to go into business battle. You'll know what you need to do and you'll know how to do it.

This book is about using two of the most powerful e-commerce tools to build a simple physical product business that you can automate as much as you want. Shopify is a platform that allows you to create online stores for anything you can sell. Shopify has so many features and services designed to make the process simple and organized for you and for your customers.

Amazon FBA is a different way of approaching the physical product business. Amazon takes care of all the logistics for you by utilizing their expansive and remarkably efficient fulfillment network with economies of scale and efficiencies we wouldn't otherwise be able to access.

Shopify

What is Shopify?

Let's start by answering a few other questions first. What is e-commerce? How long has e-commerce been around?

E-commerce is the trading of goods and services completed in an internet forum or through websites. The first use of online trading was accomplished in the early 1970s. College students made a sale using ARPANET (Advanced Research Projects Agency Network). ARPANET was founded by the U.S Department of Defense.

E-commerce has grown from that time to become a huge industry and opportunity for many! Now, let's talk about Shopify. Shopify isn't nearly as old as the internet. It was founded in Canada in 2004. Shopify started small with one company using the software platform to sell winter recreational equipment. Shopify began allowing interested individuals to create their own online stores in 2010.

The three men who started Shopify decided not to keep their success to themselves. They wanted to help other people looking to get into e-commerce web-stores.

Since its inception, Shopify has grown by leaps and bounds. Today the e-commerce empire boasts over 300,000 merchants. Online sales exceed $10M. Now it's your turn for a piece of that pie.

Now, what does Shopify do for you, the potential entrepreneur? It makes it easy for anyone with internet access to own their own online store. Shopify provides all the tools to make creating your own unique web-store a fun, exciting way to make extra money. You don't have to have the time and resources you might need if Shopify didn't exist. They have made it affordable and easy for anyone to own their own online store.

Shopify offers several ways to sell your items. You, and your customers are not limited to sitting at a laptop computer to shop. With the addition of Instagram and Twitter buying buttons, mobile apps, and other venues, your customers are never farther than a click away from your web-store.

Another neat feature of Shopify is the 24/7 vendor support. There is never a need to worry if you come across technical glitches. If you have a question, there is always someone there to help.

Shopify's blog is a great business tool. Their articles range from how to get started to how to be successful. You can read every article or pick the ones you believe will be most helpful to your business.

The culture at Shopify is geared toward great customer care. They have someone available to assist 24/7. The climate encourages great performance with frequent and noticeable recognition of employees providing excellent customer service.

Here are some questions that may come to mind while you consider opening your own Shopify web-store:

Is there a cost involved? After your 14-day free trial, you can operate your web-store for as little as $29 monthly.

Who can you talk to for ideas about how to set up and run your store? Shopify has forums with other Shopify store owners. You can also check out their tutorials. They really do make it easy for you to succeed.

You don't need to know any coding or computer language to set up or run your store. It is all made simple with plug and play tools.

Shopify is not a drop-shipping platform. You can, however, host your drop-shipping store on Shopify. Using Shopify would simplify your online presence allowing you to focus on the business of selling your products.

From Shopify's humble beginnings to its status as a multi-million-dollar e-commerce company, Shopify is a true success story. Shopify's website has a section devoted to store owners willing to share their own stories of success with the world.

So, what is Shopify? Shopify is your opportunity to get your own web-store up and running. Your chance to enter the e-commerce marketplace.

How Does Shopify Work?

It's easy to use, which is one of the reasons for its popularity. As it's a web-based software, you don't even need to install it on your computer as the platform is hosted by Shopify, which brings some key advantages, such as customer support from Shopify should anything go wrong.

No tricky installations, no inconvenient upgrades, and no worrying about web servers. It's also a software that is compatible with all operating systems, such as MacOS and Windows.

To set up an online store, you just need to sign up to Shopify and, after a 14-day free trial, you then decide which plan you want to commit to – Basic Shopify, Shopify, or Advanced Shopify – all come with different prices and key features. Once you've signed up, you simply need something to sell and a credit card to pay for the monthly costs of having Shopify, and that's it.

You can even register your own domain using Shopify, so your store will have the name you want, subject to availability. The best part is that if you have an existing website or a domain name already registered elsewhere, you can integrate it with your Shopify account, which helps provide a seamless brand experience for your customers.

What Are Some Of The Pros Of Shopify?

- ❖ One of the biggest advantages of Shopify is that it has more than 100 different storefront themes for you to choose from, allowing a professional-looking and clean image that also looks great when viewed on a mobile phone. If you've ever used WordPress before, Shopify has a similar approach to themes – there is a theme store for you to browse through where you can decide according to personal preference, to price (some are free, some are paid), or by searching for themes that are made with a certain industry in mind, such as furniture, art, or jewelry. The themes are created by professional theme designers which are then quality-checked by Shopify to ensure they are completely consistent with its software. This means you have a wide selection of professional designs at your fingertips which can really help your store to look eye-catching from the beginning.

❖ One of the other huge advantages is that it's flexible, allowing you to add functions to your store using the App Store through Shopify. With more than 1,200 different apps – some free, some paid – you can make your store more user-friendly and automated. For example, among the apps available are customer service, social media, accounting, inventory management, and shipping, which you can add to your store as tools to help you run your business. It makes Shopify more than just a store to sell goods and collect payments – it provides a complete solution to all parts of your business by offering tools to handle the back-end admin jobs too. If installing apps sounds complicated, don't worry – Shopify automatically integrates them into its software, and your store, so they're working straight away without you needing to connect them to your platform.

❖ One of the most panic-inducing moments for all online entrepreneurs is when there's a glitch in the system, making your site go down and leaving you with no idea what to do. Although Shopify is a sturdy software, in the case you do have any technical issues or just need some help, they offer an around the clock support network, so you can contact them any time. Not only that but they have several numbers you can call depending on where you are, e-mail, and an online live chat, so your problems can get addressed and resolved instantly. As a business owner, time really is money, so having access to help immediately if something goes wrong is crucial.

❖ As the Shopify software is cloud-based, it gives you a higher level of flexibility as you can use any web browser to run it. This means you can work anywhere in the world, so long as you have an internet connection.

❖ You don't need to worry about security issues as Shopify manages that side, making your payments and transactions secure, leaving you free to focus on selling.

❖ You can use the Shopify POS app (available on iOS and Android) for in-person transactions. It's a point of sale system that lets you sell anywhere such as pop-up stores, at fairs, or at markets and is versatile enough to accept a range of different payment methods. The best part is it syncs with your Shopify account, so you can keep on top of your orders and your stock levels across all your points of sale, such as your online store, retail locations, and any other sales channels that you use.

What Are Some Of The Cons Of Spotify?

Shopify has many distinct advantages that many business owners believe outweigh the cons. However, no platform is ever perfect so it's worth knowing some of the downsides, so you can make a better judgment on how it can work best for you.

❖ Unless you use Shopify payments, you will have to pay a transaction fee for every sale you make which varies between 0.5% and 2%. The variation is related to the plan you use. So, if you are on the Basic Shopify plan, you will be charged 2% of the sales value for every transaction; if you're on the Shopify plan, you will be charged 1% of the sales value; and if you're on the Advanced Shopify plan, you will be charged 0.5% of the sales value per transaction. How much of a downside this is depends on your perspective. In financial terms, it is the equivalent of $0.5 to $2 per $100 of sales made, which isn't that bad. The fee covers the cost of the technology that Shopify uses to manage the transactions, so technically you are paying for them to do the work of handling the payment. They are also transparent with their charges and make it clear what they will charge you, which can help you prepare for the bill at the end of the month.

❖ The apps we saw that can be huge advantages for your Shopify store and can really help customize your site come with a slight downside – many of them are not free and you will be charged a monthly cost to use them. The issue with this is that your monthly expenses for Shopify can add up in time, especially with the increased use of apps. Mailchimp for Shopify, for example, is an app that lets you connect Shopify to a registered Mailchimp account which lets you send targeted e-mails and highly customized ad campaigns. It's free if you have 2,000 subscribers or less but any more than this and you will need to pay a monthly fee which ranges between $10 and nearly $200. Another great app is Freshbooks, which manages the accounting side of your business yet costs $31.99 per month.

Many apps are free for low scale businesses but once your company reaches a certain size, you will have to start paying for apps that can support your store. You can see how this will begin to add up. But, it's not all so bad. As we saw, many apps are for free if you have a small business so as a new start-up, you won't need to worry about a huge financial investment. Once your business grows, the revenue will too, which means apps become more affordable. Also, tasks such as accounting and e-mail marketing need to be done anyway so you can either try doing it all yourself (not recommended as you will burn out quickly and not be able to focus on selling products to your customers as well as you should), use a different software and manually connect it to your Shopify store (which is a lot of work to say the least), hire a professional outside of Shopify who will almost certainly charge more than the app, or simply just buy the app. The great thing is that it will already be totally integrated into the platform, so you have very little work to do. It will cost you more money (although, you always have the option to not use the apps) but it will save you time and effort which you could be channeling into increasing sales.

❖ Unlike many platforms that use HTML or CSS coding, Shopify uses a code called Liquid, so if you want to customize your store, you will need to know this coding language or hire someone who does know it, which tends to be more expensive than a regular coding expert. However, you can save money in the beginning by using the themes available on

Shopify and customizing in the future once you've grown your business.

❖ Shopify is flexible and allows for high customization, yet there are some areas, such as the checkout page, that can't be changed without paying for the expensive Shopify Plus.

The key disadvantages then relate to costs, yet these are somewhat inevitable as your business grows and is a normal part of any company. For example, if you have a brick-and-mortar store, you will pay for rent, light, electricity, and all the other general costs, as well as paying staff for certain expertise such as accounting or marketing. With Shopify, the monthly fee for using the platform and the additional apps can be compared to the expenses you would have with a physical store, but are overall much cheaper.

Features On All Plans

Shopify is a complete e-commerce platform for businesses that are looking to sell their products online. While there are many options for building a webpage, and just as many online payment solutions to choose from, Shopify takes all the hassle out of mixing and matching and puts all the tools for getting your online business up and running in one place.

Additionally, Shopify is a payment gateway which means it handles the transaction verification process required to ensure that those who pay for your goods via debit or credit card have the funds to complete the purchase. It also means they are responsible for the security concerns related to these transactions which can be both complicated and expensive for merchants to pursue themselves.

When it comes to deciding how you want to use Shopify, the first thing you will need to determine is if you want to create your site and then link it Shopify or if you are more interested in getting started as quickly, easily and cheaply as possible by using the basic store template that Shopify provides. While the option to create your site will certainly cost more, it will give you complete control over the customer experience which is an important consideration if the niche you are considering working with is extremely competitive.

If you are wondering why you should use Shopify to host your e-commerce store, here are some of the features that make it a great place to open your store:

- ❖ *Unlimited products.* This basically means you can upload as many products as you want to sell in your Shopify store without any restrictions.

- ❖ *Unlimited bandwidth and online storage.* This is an important feature as it means you won't be charged for the number of visitors your store receives or for the number of photos and files you upload there.

- ❖ ***Shopify POS (point of sale).*** This is a nifty tool that allows you to make sales at a physical store (be it a pop-up shop, a market, or fair, for example) using the Shopify POS app on your iPhone or Android. The app lets you process transactions in person and manage your entire store from your Shopify account.

- ❖ ***Online sales channels.*** This allows you to use multiple sales channels, including your online store created through Shopify and any social media accounts, such as Facebook. Everything is all seamlessly integrated so it's easy to keep on top of everything and monitor your orders and transactions across all your sales channels.

- ❖ ***Fraud analysis.*** This is automatically included in Shopify payments and it helps track down orders that could be fraudulent and alert you to this risk. This is useful for you to ensure all transactions are legitimate and to avoid potential losses.

❖ ***Discount codes.*** This is a great way to drive people to your store and build up a larger audience. You may have seen influencers on Instagram who have unique codes for their fans to use with certain brands; these are the kind of codes you get with the plans. Of course, how you distribute these to your audience is up to you. In addition to asking bloggers or influencers to promote your store in exchange for something, you can also give the discount codes to first-time buyers as an incentive to buy something and use the codes as part of a targeted email campaign.

❖ ***Overview.*** Every plan gives you a rundown of your key data related to your sales. This includes overall sales, how many visitors your store is getting, and how many orders are being placed. You also get finance reports that show you your income, your payments, and any pending transactions.

❖ ***Customer service.*** You can easily contact Shopify for advice, help, or tips on their 24/7 available support network. Shopify Lite gives you access to e-mail and a live chat whereas all the other plans have a phone number you can call.

Here are some features you get on the Basic plan. They are not available on Shopify Lite, but they are also a part of the Shopify and Advanced Shopify plans.

- ❖ **Online store.** The online store is a platform that you can customize to display and sell your products. Not only is it the view your customers get of your brand, it is also the place where you can keep track of all the orders, transactions, products, and customer information related to your store. One of the best things is that it comes with a built-in website and blog, so you can run this parallel to your store and keep your products linked to informative, engaging content that helps tell your audience about what you sell, reach new customers, and get feedback on your store.

- ❖ **SSL certificate.** This is a useful tool that creates a safe connection between a browser and a server. This means that both your information and your customers' details are safe. By activating, it will show the little SSL padlock in the address bar which will give your customers a good impression and make them feel secure when shopping with you.

Features on The Shopify Plan

The Shopify plan has additional features not available on the Basic one that can really make a difference when it comes to providing a better brand experience for your customers.

❖ *Gift cards.* While discount codes are great, gift cards offer that extra bit more as they can be used on more than one visit to your site and store. It's also great to get new customers to your site, as your current customers can buy them for friends and family, who will then become your customers too. Shopify provides gift cards with various prices, so you can not only provide flexibility to your customers about how much the voucher is worth, but you can also customize the gift card to reflect your brand.

❖ *Professional reports.* These are great to help you understand the purchase behavior of your customers. These reports show sales of certain products to help you better organize the format of your store, as well as prepare for seasonal changes and plan ad and marketing campaigns. It also provides valuable information about who your customers are and how they interact with your store. For example, you can see the number of first-time visitors, the number of returning customers, who your customers are by country, and if purchases are once-off or repeated.

❖ ***Abandoned cart recovery.*** This is a feature that is definitely worth upgrading to in Shopify if it's within your budget and suitable for your business. In a nutshell, it automatically contacts customers that have placed items in the checkout but didn't end up making the purchase. By contacting them again after, you can encourage them to complete the sale. This is especially useful for stores with a high volume of traffic as this feature can significantly increase your revenue.

Features on The Advanced Shopify Plan

❖ ***Custom report builder.*** This feature lets you make unique, customized reports that let you really understand the activity on your site. For example, if you are paying for a specific ad campaign to increase traffic, you can make a report that will specifically track how that ad campaign is working for you by linking it to relevant sales and traffic. This can help you test the performance of marketing campaigns and create new strategies based on the data.

❖ **_Calculated carrier shipping._** This is a great feature that lets you integrate third-party shipping services into your store so that not only are shipping rates exact when the customer goes to purchase, you also give your shoppers a selection of different shipping options including standard delivery, express delivery, and one-day delivery.

Features You May Not Have Heard About

The above features are the basic features that each plan, depending on its level, has. However, Shopify doesn't stop there. Here are some great features that you may not have heard about.

❖ **_Customer profiles._** You can ask customers to create an account before they make a purchase. The advantage of this is that you can then track their transactions and see who your best customers are and what their purchases were. Why do you want to know this? This can help you to design highly customizable marketing campaigns for each of your customers, plan rewards for those who are most loyal and send follow up e-mails based on purchases. For example, if a customer bought a daytime moisturizer from you, you can send them a follow-up e-mail near to the time when you have estimated the moisturizer will be finishing. This gives them the chance to make a repeat purchase from you.

- ❖   ***Shopify with Facebook.*** This is handy for anyone that has a big social media following. By integrating Shopify with your Facebook account, customers can purchase directly from there, rather than having to visit your site. It makes the purchasing process much easier and more convenient for your customers, which is something that can make or break a sale. Facebook also syncs all the transactions to your Shopify account, so you can easily run everything from one platform.

- ❖   ***Drop-shipping.*** You can use your Shopify platform to run a drop-shipping store, which allows you to sell products without purchasing any inventory. The way it works is a customer buys something on your store which triggers an order to be sent to a third-party supplier who then sends the customer the product they wanted. The customer will think the product comes from you-you'll be surprised how many online stores use this model – and it means you cut all inventory costs. There are apps, such as Ordoro, which you can use to manage a drop-shipping business.

- ❖   ***Future Publishing.*** To help you better manage your time, you can use future publishing to program content to be published at specific dates and times in the future. The content remains hidden until the date you have programmed it to appear on your site. This feature means you can program weeks' or months' worth of content to appear on your site which can help you organize campaigns better.

- ❖ ***Two-step authentication.*** This gives you peace of mind that your store is safe and protected from internet hackers who could steal your password. The two-step authentication means that even if someone did steal your password, it would be incredibly difficult to enter your Shopify account as you need to sign in with your account password and enter a code that is sent to your mobile phone.

Using Shopify For Your E-Commerce Business

One of the benefits of Shopify is the ability to choose how you want to do business. Do you make quilts and want to sell them? Do you want to sell third-party products? Or maybe you want to sell a service or course? Shopify lets you do all of that and more.

You can set up a store that sells eBooks or other virtual items. Freelance writers can set up stores that sell their services, and ghostwriters can sell their words. Do you have a successful blog and want to teach others how they too can become successful? Shopify can help you set up a store to sell your courses.

Shopify also allows you to set up stores specifically for drop shipping. If a business owner has no actual product to sell, he or she can sell third-party products without having to store any inventory. This is ideal for those who are not sure what to sell or want to make some money without having to make or store any actual products.

Maybe you have some ideas on a line of clothing. You've designed your own brand and images, but you have no idea how to turn it into actual clothing. Shopify can help with that as well. Simply use a site, such as Threadless, that will turn your designs into clothing, and you can then sell that through your store without ever having to make the clothes or hold onto them.

Shopify doesn't just confine you to selling online. It also lets you sell items in person. You can purchase a card reader or use Shopify's reader to accept credit cards with your phone or tablet. Shopify makes it possible to sell in person as well as on the go so you don't have to stick with only online checkouts.

Doing business on Shopify can be easy and there are multiple ways to do it. Not only does the site simplify launching a store but it also simplifies selling your products and helps to get your business booming.

Legal Concerns

With everything moving online, there are natural concerns for the safety of information and even in the products. Does your brand actually belong to you? Is all of your private information being kept confidential? These are valid concerns, but you don't have to be too concerned.

When you set up a store, any brands or designs that you created are yours alone. No one else can take them and even if your store is closed, your brand is still your own. Your domain is also yours until you close your shop. Once closed, the domain will expire and be up for grabs again, but your brand and any designs you own are still yours.

The themes on Shopify can be borrowed by users, but are not legally theirs. In other words, go ahead and use the themes to build your brand. Should you decide to close your shop, the theme is no longer able to be used by you. The same concept applies to the domain. While you are paying for it, it is yours. If you cancel your membership, the domain will expire and you won't have rights to it anymore.

Shopify requests that all businesses post a privacy policy on the front of their store. A privacy policy ensures your customers that you will not use their information fraudulently. Your customers need to know they can trust you and that you will do your best to keep their information safe. Shopify has a policy generator that you can use to help produce a policy that will keep your customers happy.

It is important to know that while Shopify does its best to protect your privacy and information, nothing is one hundred percent safe on the internet. There is always a risk of having your private information out there on the web. Shopify is not liable for damages, including damages to products or information. If your information is hacked or stolen, this is not at the fault of Shopify and you cannot hold them responsible. This is a risk you are taking yourself. But the risk is the same as buying products on Amazon or having a membership to any other groups that might require payment. You will have to ask yourself, is the risk worth it?

While Shopify does take precautions with information and security, you can always take a proactive step and get yourself a lawyer. It can't hurt to have one for your business and to help if you are ever in trouble. Should your information be stolen or property be damaged, a lawyer can help get you back on track, and maybe even help prevent some of it.

Figuring Out What to Sell On Shopify

When it comes to creating an online store on Shopify, the first thing you are going to want to do is figure out just what it is you want to sell. Finally settling on the right product for you is immensely vital to the ultimate long-term success or failure of your store which means it should not be taken lightly. In addition to determining your profit margins, it will determine what type of marketing options are available to you which is why you should aim to find a product that fills a need in a niche that is competitive but not over full. Finding just the right mix of scarcity and demand can be difficult, but you will know it when you see it.

Market Research

Now that you have narrowed down your focus and have come up with some niche ideas, you will have to do some research. After all, your passion may be in popsicle sticks, but is there a big market for them? You will need to make sure that people want to buy what you want to sell.

Google: A simple Google search can be a great start. Google the product you're trying to sell and see how many websites are already selling it. Look through those sites and see if that product is in stock. How much is it selling for? Do people seem to be buying it? You can search for the services you offer to see how many people are also offering it and if people are buying it.

Let's say you want to offer your services as a freelance writer. A Google search for "freelance writer jobs" would produce a lot of sites for these writers. The good news is that there is a market for freelance writers, but the bad news is that the market is saturated with them. This is why the research is so important. Is it worth it to you become unique and create an amazing brand for your freelance writing services? Or is it time to find a new product to sell?

Some quick searches should show you what people want. Take a look at the most popular products being sold in the world. What are people buying up? Do you offer something similar or a little more unique? Finding out people's spending habits will give you an idea of what you can sell. Your product should be desirable without being added to an already saturated market.

Surveys: Another great way to do some research is to survey others. It sounds like a lot of work, but coming up with surveys is easy, especially if you're on social media. There are many websites that offer free surveys. You can create questionnaires asking what people think of the products you're trying to sell. Post the surveys on social media and see what people think. Twitter has an option to create polls for your post. Ask others what electronics are on their wish list, or what book they want to read next.

People are more than willing to give their opinions and this can be great for your business. If the results show that people want and like what you are trying to sell, then you are headed in the right direction.

Comparison Search: Not only is it crucial to make sure people want what you are offering but finding out more information on the actual product is equally important. Let's say you make unique, handmade baby blankets. It's a great product that people seem to be willing to buy. The next search needs to be how much others are charging for similar products. Amazon and Etsy are great sites to use to find out how much products are selling for. If Etsy shows that similar blankets are selling for fifty dollars, your prices should be around the same. Your prices need to be fair and reasonable. After all, if someone can find the same product on Amazon, but at a cheaper price, they are most likely going to spend their money on Amazon.

If you want to sell a service, check out other websites for services offered. Going back to the freelance writing service, if you were to search for freelance writing sites, you would get an idea of how much people are charging for their services. Are your prices in line with theirs? If you offer courses, make sure your class prices are similar to others' prices.

The research part of the process can be a bit tough and tedious, but it is worth it. It is important to know if you will actually sell products or if you will be lost in the sea of other similar start-ups. Finding out this information before you actually set up your shop will save you time and money.

Focus on The Demand

When it comes to finding the right items to sell, the first thing you should look for is different groups of individuals who all share a variety of similar traits. This is called a niche and finding the right one is the first step to determining what you are going to sell. When it comes to targeting the right niche, you are going to want to find one that has a fair amount of disposable income, and ideally, a hobby or interest that comes with the need to purchase lots of accessories or equipment as well. While this may sound easy, many of the obvious niches are already extremely competitive which is why it may take some thinking to find the right niche for you.

Once you find a niche that you think is not extremely competitive, the next thing you will want to determine is if there is enough of a demand for specific products in the niche in question. A market could be underserved because you got to it first, or it could be underserved because there isn't enough demand to justify the time and effort required to sell the products in question. To determine which it is, start by making a list of items that you expect to eventually sell to the niche audience in question and then take some time to search for each of them via Google.

As you are typing in each product, be on the lookout for the items that autofill into the list of suggestions as this is a great indicator of want or need in a given niche. Specifically, you want to keep an eye out for searches that indicate an unmet need when it comes to the products in question including questions about where to find or who sells the product in question. Additionally, you can find out more when it comes to unmet needs by performing the same search engine query on sites like Etsy and eBay.

Check the Competition

Once you have an idea of what items are in need in the niche, your next step should be to determine the level of competition when it comes to a specific item type. The more online stores that you find selling the same product or variations thereon the more direct competition you will have when it comes time to actually start selling products. If you can find more than 2 pages of search results selling the items you are thinking about selling with no more than a basic search you may want to consider a different niche or at least targeting a sub-niche to carve out more of a unique audience.

While checking out the competition you will want to do all of the reconnaissance to ensure that you have a good idea of what their product turnover seems to be and how robust their customer base seems to be. While scouting out the competition it is important to approach them in a rational fashion and not set out determined to crush them no matter what.

Additionally, you will want to consider the strength of any obvious competitor's social media campaigns and search engine optimization SEO. To determine how popular and effective each is, you simply need to do basic searches with terms related to the niche you are interested in entering. If a few names keep coming up again and again and again, then you may want to consider looking for a new product to sell.

Determine If Anything Is Going To Set You Apart From The Pack

Depending on what you find during your initial fact-finding mission your next step will need to be figuring out just what is going to set you and your products apart from all of the other stores that are offering similar, if not the same product. What this typically comes down to is how much personality or added value you can add to your store, to the point that it makes it preferable for customers to seek you out instead of simply jumping on Amazon for the purchase and calling it a day.

This means you will likely need to factor in additional costs, whether it is for additional items that are given away for free as incentives for single or multiple sales, or for the additional costs that will likely be accrued from creating a more personalized and unique website. If you are interested in creating a brand instead of simply selling items in an online store, then your best bet when it comes to choosing items to sell is likely going to related to a niche that you consider yourself an expert in. Generating additional content is a great way to get potential customers to your site before hopefully coercing them into a sale and having the knowledge beforehand can make content generation much easier.

Put Quality First

Once you have an idea of what types of items you are interested in selling, you will likely be tempted to start sourcing them from the cheapest vendor possible to ensure maximum profit as soon as possible. It is important to resist this urge, however, as a focus on quality will go a long way towards setting yourself apart from the pack. Especially early on when you have no other reputation to speak of, a few reviews indicating a subpar quality can be the kiss of death for a new online business. Instead of looking for the cheapest products possible, it is important to instead look for the highest quality products you can find and chalk up the difference to an early and especially effective form of marketing.

Digital Products

A majority of digital products that are sold on Shopify fall into the information category. This includes things likes software, movies, music, books, patterns, templates and more. Digital products are selling more and more every year and eBooks have actually been selling more copies than physical books since 2012.

Pros

- ❖ Digital content can be created more easily than many physical objects which limits costs significantly, specifically when it comes to manufacturing or costs related to storage.

- ❖ Shipping costs are also not a concern because digital items can be sent electronically and customers can be using their products minutes after purchasing them.

- ❖ These other benefits combine to create much higher profit margins on average when it comes to digital as opposed to physical items, even though the physical items typical cost much more.

Cons

❖ Piracy poses a significant threat to all types of digital content as once it has been pirated its value drops to practically 0 in nearly all instances.

❖ The digital quality of more complicated digital files is limited by the common use infrastructure that limits the size of practical files.

❖ Certain items simply cannot have a digital-analog which makes the digital market inherently limited to a few specific fields.

❖ The current quality limitations of technology ensure that physical copies of media will currently always look or sound better than digital alternatives.

Physical Products

When it comes to selling items on Shopify, physical goods still outnumber digital goods to a significant degree. Though much of this market is controlled by global brands, the percentage of this trillion-dollar market that small business is expected to control is estimated to be on the rise and may grow by more than 40 percent in the next 5 years.

Pros

❖ Psychologically, many people, especially those of older generations, are simply more comfortable paying for physical as opposed to digital goods which means that every physical goods deal will be easier to sell, at least for now.

❖ Physical products are also still unilaterally trusted more than their digital counterparts. Many of the stigmas from the early days of the internet remain, including that downloaded products are more likely to work incorrectly than their physical counterparts.

❖ If you decide to sell physical products, you will have access to a much wider variety of products as well as distributors of products to choose from.

Cons

❖ Physical products are always going to incur costs at every step of the way, production costs, shipping costs, storage costs and generally another round of shipping costs are all often required. This typically results in a lower profit margin as well.

❖ Some physical products cannot be shipped to certain areas and other items cannot be shipped at all due to their delicate nature. All the concerns related to an item's sheer physicality are all on this list as well.

Subscription Products

One of the more recent e-commerce trends: if you use your Shopify account to sell a subscription service then you are getting people to promise to pay you a set amount each month in exchange for a predetermined level of products that are automatically sent out at a specific period of time. The items are niche specific, but generally, the exact makeup of each monthly purchase is determined by the seller which means a subscription model can be quite profitable when utilized properly.

Pros

❖ Subscription boxes automatically generate customer loyalty by forcing customers to commit to an implied long-term relationship right up front.

❖ It can be easy to build an initial customer base as it is easy for customers to buy in at the promise of trying something new.

❖ Complete brand control over an entire product line.

❖ Great choice for products that naturally wear out somewhat quickly after regular use.

Cons

❖ Regardless of the items in question, subscriptions are often seen as luxury items which means they are the first things cut during the financial crisis.

❖ Ensuring that reoccurring billing is correct can be extremely difficult as customers often won't think of such services until the payment has already failed to go through.

❖ If the cost from the supplier changes unexpectedly you are still on the hook for the agreed upon amount.

Services

Although less common, you can sell services online such as web design, web development, writing services, and consulting. It's a great way of building a network of loyal clients, but it's hard to scale in the beginning unless you start employing other staff.

You can sell any of these goods – physical, digital, or services – on Shopify.

Getting Your Products

Another important thing to consider when planning your business model is where will your products come from? You have a few different options.

❖ Make them. You can make your products yourself, which is common if it's organic clothing, natural beauty products, or tailor-made cakes. While the obvious issues of doing this yourself include difficulty in making your business big and the intense time commitment, it does mean you have total control over what is being sold. If you make them, you need to consider the costs of the raw materials and the cost of storing them.

❖ Manufacture them. The alternative option is to get someone to make the item for you by sourcing your products from manufacturers. You can either search for a domestic manufacturer (usually more expensive) or an overseas manufacturer (often cheaper).

❖ Wholesale. This is when you buy products directly from a supplier or manufacturer, usually at a cheaper price. Then, you sell it for a much higher price. This is a less risky business model than making it or manufacturing it yourself as you don't need to purchase such high volumes of the product.

❖ Drop-shipping. This is becoming an increasingly popular business model. You sell products on your store, but you don't actually have any inventory. When a customer makes a purchase on your store, an order will be sent to the supplier or drop-shipper. Then, they will send the product directly to your customer. This means you don't need to worry about storing products or shipping costs. The profits you make are the difference between what you charge your customer and what the supplier or drop-shipper charges you. It sounds like a great business model and it really is; however, profit margins are often very small or even tiny in highly competitive areas, and you have to make sure you choose your drop-shipping partner or supplier carefully. One of the most popular Shopify apps for drop-shipping is Oberlo, which gives you access to thousands of different suppliers.

All of these business models are compatible with Shopify and the one you choose will depend on your product and how you want to sell it.

Setting up Your Shopify Store

Getting your Shopify store up and running is very easy and Shopify will walk you through the entire process. First head to their website and click on "Get Started". This will take you to the sign-up page where you will enter your email and password. Then you will choose your shop name. After a few brief questions about you and your shop, you can open your store. You can sign up for a free trial to start, just to make sure that this is what you want.

After giving your information, Shopify will take you to a dashboard page where you will be able to customize and set up your shop. Shopify will walk you through all of it. You'll need to select a plan for your shop, but you won't be charged until after your trial is over. If you cancel before the trial is up, you will not be charged.

Set up a Product: Start on the home page and create your first product. Choose a name for your product, upload images, add descriptions, and set a price. You can add shipping if it's a physical product you are selling, and you can even set up a "compare at" price to compare your cost to other similar products. Does your product have a variant (other colors or sizes)? You can add that as well.

Choose a Theme: Your next step on the home page to set up a theme so that your store has the look you need. If you would like to see the themes available through Shopify, simply click "upload theme" and then "Shopify Theme Store". You will see that some themes are free while others cost a certain amount of money. If you're just starting out, go ahead and choose a free theme for now. There is not much risk in losing money and you can always go back and change your theme. Once you have found a theme, simply click on it and install it.

Choose a Domain: Shopify will automatically assign you a domain name with their name attached to it. If you want your own domain name you will have to set that up as well. Different domains will cost different amounts of money, with .coms costing around fourteen dollars. Having a good domain is important because you want to grab your customer's attention. And while the free domain provided can work if you are on a tight budget, it is recommended to buy a new domain that doesn't have the Shopify name in it. This way, the shop looks more professional and your customers know the site is yours. And if you already have a domain name, that's great! You can transfer it over to your Shopify store easily.

Two-Step Authentication: While setting up your store, be sure to also set up the "two-step authentication". This will keep your account safe by generating unique codes that only you can use should a problem arise. This also makes you use a code when you sign in. Shopify sends you a six-digit code to use when you sign in, making it much harder for just anyone to access your account.

Should you choose, this is also a good time to set up your profile. Simply head over to your account page and set up your profile. There, you can write your bio and give customers an idea of who you are and what you do. You can also upload a picture of yourself. This will give customers a face for the store and makes shopping a more personal experience.

Shipping: On your homepage, you will also see that you can set up shipping costs. Shipping can be calculated at checkout according to your shipping policies. You can choose the regions you ship to, whether that's local or worldwide, and set pricing for those regions. Having shipping profiles set up makes it easier to use them when posting new products for sale in your shop. You can also buy and print shipping labels to make things easier for your online business.

Set up a Buy Button: Once you have a few products, you'll want to also set up a buy button. Having a buy button widget will make it easy for customers to see and purchase your products from a wide variety of sites. Let's say you also run a blog, and in an article, you are advertising a product you sell. You can add that buy button to your blog post so that customers can click it and be taken right to your store. This button will work with a variety of websites including Tumblr and Squarespace. Shopify will walk you through the process of setting up the widget and getting it embedded into other sites.

Comparison Tool: Next, you will want to take advantage of Shopify's comparison tool. This is located toward the bottom of the homepage. Here, you can describe what you are selling and Shopify will compare it to other similar items. They will let you know how your items compared to others out there. Can your items compete with a mass of similar items? Or are yours so unique they really stand out from the crowd?

While setting up your Shopify store and account, you will notice that there are "cards", or little links to helpful information. It is a good idea to click on some of these as they have a wealth of good information on how to start a business. The articles will teach you how to start and grow your business with tips and tricks the most successful entrepreneurs use. One article discusses gathering your audience before opening your shop in order to secure excited customers before the shop even opens. They are also quick reads, so don't worry about this taking up a lot of our time. These articles are, however, worth your time because of the valuable content they have.

Customizing Your Shopify Store

By now, you should have a great shop set up. We've gone over the basics of getting your online store up and running, but now it's time to customize. Your shop should be unique to you and you'll want to run it in a way that makes it easy to manage.

If you haven't already chosen your theme, take this time to shop around for one that is perfect for what you are looking for. You have the option of exploring free themes or premium themes. If you have the means to buy yourself a premium theme, it is well worth it. The premium themes allow you to customize more. If you are just starting off and don't have the funds to invest in themes yet, there are still plenty of free options available that look just as nice. Here we will explore what you can do with free and premium themes.

Free Themes

There are a lot of free themes that are available on Shopify, and all of them are truly worthwhile. To start choosing and customizing the theme of your shop, simply click on "Explore Free Themes". Here you will find different styles of themes. If you want something simple for your shop, use the Simple styles. If you need something a little more glamorous, try the Venture or Debut styles.

The Simple theme is perfect if you are selling multiple products and really want to focus in on that alone. Themes like Pop and Venture really showcase the images more and make your shop stand out. With some really great photography, these themes can really stand out from the crowds. Narrative and Boundless are set up to look more like a blog. This can be really useful for those looking to sell services.

Premium Themes

Premium themes can be very helpful to your business. They are more customizable and add "pop" to your shop. You can choose a theme based on what you are selling or one based on how you want the layout to look. For example, the theme Expression has four different styles that you can choose from. Each style is unique and expressive. Once you click on a style, you will see how it looks and can even see a free preview of what your shop would look like with that theme. Themes like Startup are more for shops with low inventory. If you only have a few items to sell, this theme is perfect for you. It's designed to showcase one thing at a time so that it is not obvious that there are not a lot of items in the shop.

Customization

Once you have chosen a theme and downloaded it, you will need to customize it. Simply click on "Customize

Theme" and you will be directed to the customization page. Here you will be able to change and modify the theme as needed. Customization pages may be different depending on the theme you have chosen. Some premium themes may have more options. They will all, however, have many similar concepts.

Logo: You will want to set up a logo for your shop. Your logo can be as simple as a picture of a product, but really it should showcase what your shop it. You can design one easily on photo apps or websites. Many offer free picture designs that you can use as a logo. PicMonkey is a favorite app among bloggers because it has many free features that can help you come up with a logo, or you can also try Photoshop or other websites. Of course, you do not need a logo. Should you choose not to use one, your shop's name will appear at the top of the page instead of a logo image. And this can look nice and simple as well.

Featured Image: Next you will want to set up a few featured images. These images should stand out. It would be helpful to either use a professional photographer or take the time to learn how to take professional looking pictures. There are many sites that offer tutorials. The website Improve Photography has a lot of free tips on how to make your photos look more professional.

Slideshows: Some themes offer slideshows while others offer a featured image. You can upload your own image or use one of Shopify's many stock images. You can also choose to have a text overlay on many images. Experiment with these options so that you can see the different ways to make the images and headings look unique to your shop.

Collections: You can also now set up your collections and the way that your inventory is displayed in your shop. For some themes, this may be simple images. For others, this may be setting up the page like a traditional store with images and prices under that. When you chose your theme, you probably already had an idea of how you wanted the layout of your products to look. This is a good time to play around with the layout and set it up to achieve your image goals.

You can add collections and categories so that your products are organized how you want. If you're selling electronics, you can organize your products into categories such as "Headphones" and "Chargers". If you are selling your freelance writing services, you could have collections such as "Blog Posts", "eBooks Written", or "Writing Samples". Giving your products categories helps customers find what they are looking for faster and easier because everything will be organized neatly into their own category.

Images: You can insert more images to go along with your page to add to the outward appeal of the shop. Play around with adding extra pictures or text. You could set up a picture of you on the page with text overlay describing a bit about you. This will give customers an idea of who they are buying from without actually looking at any About information (let's face it, lots of people just want products and don't always care to look at an About page). Instead of using your own image, you can use a stock image with a text overlay describing a recent customer testimonial. This will let customers know that you already have a loyal clientele and that they are satisfied customers.

General Settings: Within the customization page for your theme, you will also find the general settings. Here you can modify the color scheme of your theme and the fonts used. You can also choose the size of your font and how your checkout will look. You can add more images here and also link your social media accounts. Linking your social media can be exceptionally beneficial to your business. People like knowing who they are buying from. Social media gives the customer a truer look into who you are and what your business is about. It also provides you with places to update customers on the latest things happening in your shop.

Apps: While it is important to customize the theme of your shop, there are also more ways to customize the actual shop to make things run smoother for you. Adding apps can really help your business. Apps like Oberlo help you to sell third-party products and get your dropshipping going. Printful is an app that will print your designs and get them shipped for you. There are apps to help you with social media and sales and marketing. Search through available apps and find which ones will help you to become more successful.

Blogs: You can also create blog posts with Shopify. This is a useful tool for your business. Blog posts can consist of anything on your mind, or promotions, or thoughts on products in your store. Keeping a blog going gives customers more insight into what you are selling or what you will be selling. It makes your store more personal and shows customers you are a human being as opposed to just another program just selling things.

Pages: Adding pages can help get your site noticed more. Have multiple pages focused on different aspects of your store. Create an about page that really delves into who you are, what you believe in, your values, and what your store is about. Create a page for certain types of services or items. With clear page titles that are descriptive, you can help customers find their way to your store.

Home Page: The home page doesn't have to be called Home, either. If you look under the Preferences section while customizing your store, you will find that you can rename your home page. You can also give it a description that will help customers find your home page. This section uses search engine optimization techniques. If your store is set up to help others redecorate, you can use wording that would appeal to your ideal customer. Use words the customer would search for such as "redecorate", "room ideas", or simply "new curtains".

More Settings: The Settings area also has some customization tools for your shop. Here you can choose your time zone, set up the legal name for your shop, or change your email. In the Payment section you can set up the methods you will accept for payment. You can link your PayPal account, set up manual payment options, and add other payment options such as Amazon Pay or BitPay. The checkout methods can be customized as well. You can choose how the checkout process will go and which information will be required upon checkout. You can customize how people will find your products, such as sell buttons or directly through your store. The way taxes are applied can be customized and you can set up what notification to activate and how you want to send them out. The Settings section has a lot of information and items to go through. It is recommended that you explore this section and modify each setting to suit your needs.

As you can see, there are a lot of ways to customize your store. It may be intimidating with so many options, but if you take the time to explore them, you will see that it gets easier. Customizing your site gives the outward appearance some character that defines your store. Customizing the details can help your store run as smooth as possible, allowing you to work less.

Expanding Your Product Line

Once you have finally gotten everything up and rolling there is nothing left to do but market your products and find customers. Eventually, you are going to feel the need to begin expanding the types of products that your store sells, and in doing so you will open yourself up to many new questions and concerns.

Adding products tactically

The life cycle of the products on your page can be seen as being in one of four primary cycles. The startup phase is when a product first comes on the market and you are building awareness of it. The second is growth when sales of that particular product are growing the most; this is followed by maturity when the product begins to regularly sell an expected amount of units. Finally, the maturity stage is then sometimes followed by the exit stage is when the interest for the product is in a decline. While not every product hits all the stages, when a product begins to decline in sales you need to know what to do.

When you are ready to start expanding your stock, what you need to do is look at the analytics and determine just which of your products are producing the most consistent conversions. From there, it is simply a matter of analyzing the data and determining if adding another similar item would likely split the number of sales or if it is likely to double them. If this does not appear to be a step in the right direction, instead it might be better to determine why interest has dropped off on the product in question. Many of the common reasons for a product's decline have to do with a newer version being released or a change in the practices related to how that product is made or used. If this is the case, then something as simple as a few minutes' research can totally refresh your product line.

Find out what your customers want by including a survey regarding a product expansion in an email newsletter. There is nothing to be gained by beating around the bush in this instance and because only your best customers are likely going to interact with your newsletter, you have a way to directly ask your target audience what they want to buy from you. Take the time to draft up a realistic grouping of new products and also leave room for a write-in section, you may be surprised at the results you find.

Finding new products
When it comes to looking for new products to sell, the first thing you are going to want to do is to take a look at your existing stock and see if there are any obvious holes in your product line. If nothing sticks out to you at this point, your next best bet is likely to be to get offline and out into the world of brick and mortar retail stores. Take the time to seek out local variations on the theme of your niche and you might be surprised at how easily a new product idea or service comes to mind.

Back online, another viable alternative that more and more online stores are embracing is the world of Kickstarter manufacturers. Finding niche relevant content in this area is as easy as going to Kickstarter.com and looking through successfully funded Kickstarter pages to find products that might speak to your niche. Getting in touch with these types of manufacturers can often lead to a mutually beneficial relationship wherein they get a way to sell their product once they have delivered on their initial backer promises and you get an exclusive item that there is a proven demand for.

With that being said, it is important to ensure that the demand in question hasn't burned out with the fulfillment of the Kickstarter campaign. Do some research and search out any additional demand for the product, (the faster the better) because if you don't meet the demand someone else will. While forming a good relationship with a Kickstarter manufacturer can lead to great things, it is important to do your research and only deal with manufacturers who have already successfully shipped product.

The great thing about Kickstarter is that anyone with an idea can get it funded, but this means that oftentimes people need to adapt to new roles on the fly which can be more difficult than it might first appear. Ensuring that the company has shipped product first will go a long way towards weeding out many of the problems inherent in the early days of a manufacturing company. Regardless, it is important to never offer to pay for exclusivity and to always get everything in writing as you will not be able to completely rely on the company until they have sent you a few shipments of products.

FBA

What Is Amazon Fba?

Amazon is known to be the largest global online retailer, which is a preferred market platform by many people to sell their products online. Amazon helps boost sales with its world-class fulfillment and expertise. Sellers can leverage their Fulfillment process where Amazon handles the logistics: they pick, pack, and ship orders to customers. It became an income-generating venue for third-party sellers or merchants who want to make passive income through selling products online.

Of course, it's not only the manufacturers and online business owners who can sell on Amazon to help grow their sales. If you're looking for REAL online business, Amazon has a potential to earn you a steady income for life.

Selling on Amazon can earn income with just a few products or you can take advantage of building a business with more than 20 categories of products to list. It's a big and exciting place for online sellers to widen their customer reach and increase their sales.

Is Amazon FBA the right platform for you?

Now that we have been talking about how the Amazon FBA program is so great, it may seem redundant to you if we tell you to ask yourself, "Is this program going to be good for me?"

Each business has its own specific dynamics and it is important at this stage to check if the product lines you have selected and the target audience for those products will be active on Amazon. You want to leverage FBA if you believe your product will sell well on Amazon. Since amazon has positioned themselves as the "everything store," there are no longer closely defined product categories that are bought and sold on Amazon. Amazon is constantly expanding its product offering, so chances are, products like yours already are selling on Amazon.

However, different businesses have different needs, and not all products are good for Amazon FBA.

There is no such thing as an objective advantage nor is there such a thing as an objective disadvantage-this is especially true in the world of business. An advantage could rapidly deteriorate into a disadvantage if you do not know how to make it work well for you. Likewise, an apparent disadvantage or maybe even something neutral could quickly become an advantage after taking a few considerations and making a few changes. What works for you may not work for another and what works for one product may hurt the sales of another.

Successful people always make informed decisions and once they have done so, they make sure that they carry the momentum through.

That said, the best answer to the above question of whether Amazon FBA is good for you is (like with most things in life): It depends.

It Depends…What are you selling?

The nature of what you are selling is of huge importance. There are fixed fees and variable fees associated with Amazon FBA; pick and pack handling fees stay the same whereas other fees vary with weight and size. Thus, if items are relatively small, not too heavy, and sell at higher prices, it makes the FBA fees more manageable. If what you sell falls under this category, then Amazon FBA may be very profitable for you.

Take as an example: the FBA fees charged for a $10 item that is large and heavy will take a big bite out of your margin, whereas the FBA fees for a much smaller and lighter item that sells at $35 will represent a much smaller percentage of the revenue cut.

The second smaller lighter item makes more sense for a number of reasons: the small size and weight represent smaller fees, but even more, its high average sale price (the average price at which the item is sold across different markets) poses an even bigger incentive to put this product category out into the market. Simply put, a smaller lighter product with a higher price will offer excellent returns on the investment you have made of money and effort.

Jewelry is a good example of a small, light, item with a high average sale price.

Another thing to consider is the popularity of a product. To cut a long story short, you do not want to send a product that gets stuck at the Amazon warehouse racking up storage fees.

You want to put up popular items that sell. Although a school of thought exists that proposes that items that rank lower in sales have a high chance of doing well on FBA due to the incentives and perks ushered in by Amazon Prime, there is still some risk—enough risk to warrant some thought from the seller before any decision is made.

This means that once you have signed on and you're ready to go, it is prudent to take some time and do some basic mathematics. The results may just surprise you.

In short RESEARCH. You are looking for the right products at the right price and the right quality. Time spent here will get you the results.

It Depends…How Much Do You Sell?

After thinking through the above-mentioned decisions the next stage is to work out the scale you wish to have. If you are dealing with a lot of inventory, then FBA is definitely an attractive option to look at because it helps you with storage and logistics. The higher your turnover rate, the more storage space Amazon is willing to grant you.

On the other side of the scale maybe a beginner is not sure and is only looking at a modest start at a smaller scale just to test the waters and then see if he can do it. In this case too, people just starting out in business can benefit from the FBA service as they could practically hand over the support tasks to Amazon and concentrate on growing their business. In such cases even if the profit margins are not that high and Sales may be a little slow to start with, a seller is saved the usual hassles of Order fulfillment.

This means Amazon FBA presents a good fit for businesses that produce either on a high level, are on the rise in volumes of production and beginners especially when the framework necessary for handling this amount is not in place or is still in the process of being set up.

Good customer reviews are very important especially in the online business models and by using Amazon FBA you can rest assured that the risk of getting negative reviews is countered by ample opportunities to get positive reviews.

With Amazon on your team, you are safe and can be confident that customer satisfaction is taken care of.

It Depends…How Much Man Power Do You Command?

However lean you may want to keep your business and whatever automation you may incorporate, the truth is that ultimately for even small matters you will require some manpower. This manpower requirement at times may just be required in times of a surge in sales, let's say in the festive season. For a small business owner, handling this can become a major headache.

Businesses inevitably experience a point where demand increases either as a result of the natural growth process or as a result of the time of year or season. Fulfilling an item yourself means, making sure that the packaging is of a very high standard, and then involves going to the post office, or engaging with a shipping carrier for each item or each order. The speed of execution expected by customers these days adds an extra worry. Sometimes you might need some help in such a scenario which will only add to your expenses.

Amazon FBA is a great way to offset the cost of manpower needed to cope with both the regular day to day order fulfillment tasks as well as an overabundance of demand when orders pour in.

If, on the other hand, you have adequate staff and help which can cope with the occasional increase in demand, then maybe the extra cost incurred for Amazon doing these things for you is unnecessary.

However, if you do have a need, then FBA provides a solution to the problem of the cost of hiring and the stress of managing additional manpower. Fulfillment by Amazon may also be useful if you find it hard to predict when there will be a surge in demand, and therefore cannot prepare the necessary manpower or put the necessary framework in place.

So is FBA worth the effort for your business ambitions? Only the seller, with his business in mind, can answer that. The most effective advice one can get is: Know your business.

To be more specific, however, your business is not good for Amazon FBA if one or more of the following is true:

- Low volume, low margin:

- You have selected a product or set of products which have a small niche market. This will usually mean that though you will sell, the volumes are going to be slow and low.

As with all decisions you have to make, this one is totally yours.

Remember that it is a decision which means that the built-in costs of the Amazon FBA program will prove to be a major handicap for your business if your margin is too low. If you can barely scrape a profit without the FBA fees, the revenues which you generate will not be sufficient to meet the costs and still give you a profit.

If this is the case, you do not need to sign on to the Amazon FBA program and will be better off if you handle the Order fulfillment part yourself.

The silver lining, in this case, is that as the order volumes are not that high you can spend time in a productive manner by ensuring that personal attention is given by you to each order you get and you have total control on the process.

Therefore, you need to ensure that the order is packaged properly, and the item gets shipped immediately. It will also help if you get personally involved in customer service if and when the need arises.

Selling heavy and inexpensive or large, low-margin items:

Larger and bulkier items simply need more storage space. They also require more handling and packaging as well as higher costs while shipping. Remember you will be paying to ship them first to Amazon and then the higher cost of shipping to the customer will be indirectly charged to you.

These larger items may also be slow to sell and all this time you will be paying Amazon while they sit on the shelf.

The higher FBA fees and charges can seriously eat up your profit if you're not careful with the selection of your product portfolio.

I am sure with this information you will be able to decide what works for you.

Cannot invest upfront capital in inventory:

By now you must have understood that in the Amazon FBA program you have to source and purchase enough items in order to build up your inventory. Then this inventory needs to be sent across to Amazon for storage and processing.

You do need a fair amount of capital to be able to build up an inventory which is going to give you enough sales and then profit.

Which means you need to set a goal, save and build a good amount in order to invest in creating this inventory. If you have a decent amount saved with you, they might as well put it to good use by joining the Amazon FBA program.

On the flip side, this means that once have a fairly good amount of capital you are effectively barring quite a few competitors leaving you enough room to get those customers.

Why People Pay More on Amazon?

Amazon has built a great reputation for almost 18 years now. They continuously develop programs, especially for their customers. With the current program, Amazon Prime, customers are valued with numerous benefits by becoming a Prime member.

Isn't it a good idea to sell products where your customers can enjoy these benefits from Amazon? Your customers can benefit from the following:

> ➢ Free 2-day shipping

> ➢ Unlimited deliveries with no minimum order size

➢ Unlimited movies and shows with Prime Instant Video

➢ Unlimited video streaming and photo storage

➢ Early access on Amazon Lightning deals and MyHabit.com

➢ Collection of free e-books with one book a month borrowed (no due date)

➢ Discounted automatic delivery (some most used items)

➢ Hassle-free returns

It's important to consider that not everyone is totally price conscious. Amazon.com caters to all people who prefer online convenience when getting a product they need, even if they are non-Prime members. For some busy professionals, to have the convenience of getting a product shipped to their doors could be advantageous even with a little extra cost to spend on the item. For a snowed-in family, the extra $3.99 shipment fee is worth the cost than to go out of their house during the cold season just to buy an item they want. Also, persons living in the country would rather pay an extra fee, instead of driving an hour, each way, to get an item. If you think about it, the cost and time they spend to commute and purchase an item are the same cost they spend with Amazon, but with the added benefit of saving them time.

People buy on Amazon because of the service of shipping the product. Definitely, the convenience of receiving the item right at the doorsteps makes a difference to the customers.

Selling on Amazon is a great way for you to sell products on a network with a great reputation and have millions of established buyers. With its marketplace, there is a big chance to make a profit from selling products. Indeed, selling products on Amazon is an opportunity to reach more customers globally.

Aside from **the advantage of Amazon's marketplace**, sellers are guaranteed the following:

1. Friendly selling experience.

Amazon has the most user-friendly database. You'll discover how easy it is in this book.

2. Huge products database with detailed item information.

This makes the Amazon Store a quick venue to sell products showing detailed enticing information to the prospective buyers.

3. Pay sellers on time.

When making payments, Amazon is reliable and does it on time.

4. Easier selling with the FBA program.

Amazon Store creates an easy platform and fulfillment services by providing the complete selling resources such as warehousing and logistics, which makes selling on Amazon easier and more reliable.

The Features And Advantages Of Selling On Amazon, The Fulfillment By Amazon (FBA) Program.

The small cost of joining Amazon FBA is worth the benefits that a seller could get from it. Here are some advantages of selling on Amazon FBA:

- Time is saved in sending items by order

- Amazon takes care of the inventory

- Amazon does the right packaging to fill daily orders

- Customer service is done by Amazon, including refunds/returns

Amazon offers the FBA program to eliminate fulfillment difficulties of online sellers and helps to level up the business. Amazon sellers have experienced huge increases in the money they make, sales growth and customer satisfaction. Most of the Amazon sellers have reached a 20% incremental increase in their sales when they joined FBA.

Amazon Selling Options

Amazon offers different ways to sell products in their marketplace. To differentiate the options, here are the two ways of Amazon selling:

1. Sell products TO Amazon

Selling to Amazon is an invite program to sell products directly to Amazon where you are granting Amazon the ownership of your inventory. Amazon will then market and sell to shoppers on Amazon.com.

You must take note that if you choose to be a supplier to Amazon, you're selling your products at wholesale rates. Granting Amazon the full ownership of the products and letting them choose their own price and shipping options for the products. This selling option need not to use the Amazon FBA service.

Although becoming a supplier may mean you will be getting lower rates for your items, it may benefit you by eliminating tasks such as marketing, advertising, and pricing.

2.   Selling ON Amazon

This selling option is what we call Amazon FBA. When you sell on Amazon, you have greater levels of control and potentially higher margins on your listed products on Amazon. Unlike selling to Amazon as a supplier, this option allows you to control shipping, prices, and order fulfillment.

Here are the advantages of selling on Amazon:

1.   **Find New Customers.**

With the huge marketplace of Amazon, sellers can gain exposure to new and varied customers. Prime members see your products as eligible for free two-day shipping which customers normally prefer a short delivery lead time at no cost.

2.   **Capitalize on Amazon's Branding.**

Sellers can leverage the marketplace benefits by capitalizing on Amazon's branding as the largest online shopping destination. Listing products on a marketplace known for its ease of online selection and shopping, as well as its reliability, can benefit a seller. Remember: nobody trusts a random online retailer, who they can't see or talk to. So, the best thing people can do is sell through companies with a great reputation and branding, such as Amazon.

3. Increase Sales.

Sellers who own an online store are taking advantage of the increased exposure on Amazon. Your products can gain visibility with millions of customers. This exposure eventually translates to increased sales through Amazon's marketplace especially when customers can view your listings labeled with Amazon delivery guarantee.

So, which option gives you the highest levels of profit?

I'd rather tell you, it's selling ON Amazon! The truth is, it is more popular than selling to Amazon as a supplier.

The wide coverage of Amazon is another reason that Amazon FBA is the best option for selling your products online with global opportunity. Also, its features and services are highly flexible.

Sellers do not need to live in the United States to get a chance of growing a business. With the global marketplace of Amazon, they make the FBA program possible to different countries.

At this time, aside from the United States, FBA is available in countries like the United Kingdom, Canada, France, Italy, Germany, China, Japan, Spain, Mexico, and India. There are fulfillment centers in these countries. Surely, Amazon can offer FBA to more countries in the next few years.

So, why not sell on Amazon with the FBA program?

Lack of experience and capital should not stop you from starting your online selling business. The Amazon FBA business model is designed so unique to help even an average seller.

What's more, Amazon finds ways to make sure that they provide the sellers with great tools and resources in leveraging the selling business.

For example, would you like to know Amazon's selling rate of an item before you decide to start selling that item on Amazon?

Definitely, that piece of information will be useful when you have the answer. Having the indication of an item's recent high sales on Amazon can help in your buying decisions.

To find this information, I can refer you to Amazon Best Seller Rank.

The Sales Rank report is just a snapshot of ranks in time and not the total of quantity sold from the time an item is listed on Amazon.

For example, two items may have the same Sales Rank that both sold one unit at a particular time, even if one of the items only sold one unit per month for 2 years and the other have just sold only one unit after 2 years. The Sales Rank of the two items only indicates that the items are sold recently.

Sales Rank gradually gets higher and higher whenever the item sells again. Amazon updates Sales Rank every hour. You can try to observe how an item changes its rank to get a broader view of how a product sells.

But, you should not think that those items with lower rank aren't selling well. Observe how its rank spikes from time to time that indicates it is being sold frequently. Ironically, the lower rank indicates that the item is quicker to expect a sale. You'll notice how an item changes its rank in a short period of time.

How Selling on Amazon Works?

Selling on Amazon works for two different types of sellers according to the subscribed plan, which is as Professional or Individual Seller. Signing up and choosing the plan to start as an Amazon seller is discussed in the next chapter. These two selling plans offer you the flexibility to sell one or a thousand items.

Before that, I want to give you a clear guide on how selling on Amazon works: there is a 4-step process to follow once registered:

Step 1: List products.
If you're an individual seller, you add products to the Amazon catalog one at a time, unlike the Professional subscription that allows you to add batches of items. If the product is already on Amazon.com, just take note of the quantity, condition and shipping options for the products you have to sell. For unlisted products on Amazon.com, you need to identify the UPC (Universal Product Code) and SKU (Stock Keeping Unit) and prepare products attributes like title, description, and product images.

Step 2: Sell to Customers.
Listing your products will automatically make them available on Amazon.com for customers when they search for products related to yours. The service of Amazon starts from here where you have placed your item on a trusted marketplace. Amazon will notify you whenever there is a successful order. Set your account settings on which method you want to be notified, either by email or text message.

Step 3: Ship Order.

If an item is sold, Amazon will notify you that a customer placed an order. Using the Amazon FBA Program will let Amazon do the shipping of your ordered item. This is a hassle-free fulfillment of customer's order. On the other hand, you can choose fulfillment by the merchant, which allows you to process shipment details but may cause you headaches.

Step 4: Get Paid.

Amazon will pay you on a regular schedule, generally every 14 days. There is nothing to worry about because you will be notified whenever they deposit payments on your bank account. You need to provide valid information for your bank account. Just maintain a minimum of $1 in your Amazon account balance for disbursements to take place.

As a cost-effective program, you only pay as you go. You're only charged for the storage space and orders they fulfill.

Certainly, the Amazon FBA program is a good deal for online sellers!

You have just learned the essential information about selling online on Amazon using the Fulfillment by Amazon program. Now you have the option to sell with fewer headaches and effectively streamline the running of your business, and eventually, have more time to focus on how your business can grow.

E-Commerce Redefined

How to Get Started

Most of the people reading this book may have little to no experience selling online. That is by all means okay. We are all here to learn, are we not? The first step in getting started is being familiar with the Amazon experience. This entails getting a decent if not an impeccable understanding of how the Amazon system works, selling and pricing products. Here a few things you may need to know about Amazon. Feel free to do comparisons with other e-commerce platforms.

- Listing on Amazon is free of charge. Charges are only paid upon sales.

- Amazon uses debit, credit, and their gift cards for payment purposes. Amazon then makes the payment to the seller thus the platform has no occurrence of unpaid items.

- Amazon matches the ISBN number on media products or UPC codes to their built-in product page. This eases listing products on Amazon.

- Amazon has no option to contact sellers with questions. The platform handles customer service.

- It is not possible to block potential buyers on Amazon.

- A seller on Amazon has to be personally keen on the Sales Rank since no research tool is associated with the site.

- All items that are purchased must be shipped in 2 business days from the date of sale.

- All sold items on Amazon have a money-back guarantee within 30 days.

- Feedback on Amazon is not particularly important. Only 5% of customers utilize the feedback system.

- Approval is required for sellers to list and sell in all restricted categories such as cell phones, electronics, computers, software, jewelry, and clothing. This is to ensure sellers meet and qualify performance standards.

For those who may never have sold on Amazon before, I would suggest you start with media products before going non-media. Why? Because:

1. Books, CDs, and DVDs are in everyone's home. Selling items that are in your possession already generate enough income to purchase more inventory with time.

2. Most of these products are more often than not low-priced. The platform does impose a selling limit for beginners. You do not want to be on

listing restriction or probation while new in your venture. I suggest listing and selling media products for about 30 days before venturing further. Remember patience is key to achieving success in FBA.

3. Learn how to handle items that are merchant filled before scaling up to FBA. This means shipping the purchased items yourself. This does come in handy when time may run short while you have some fast sellers on your hands. It could also help sell inventory that is not viable, yet profitable, to be sold through FBA. These may include aerosol can products, hazardous or flammable products such as perfumes.

Before getting started on the actual business, there are a couple of basic Amazon concepts that you are expected to comprehensively understand. While this is mainly done by gathering as much information as possible, rest assured that gaining the familiarity comes with practice. The more time you spend on the platform, the easier your grasp and understanding of the basics.

The Seller Central.

This page brushes up on the basic information required for one to sell conveniently on Amazon. This could be a tad redundant for those who are already familiar with the concept. A quick review would not hurt either, would it?

Before making any sales on Amazon, you do need to have a Seller Central Account. I would recommend that you create a "Professional" Seller Account. This costs $40 every month with the first 30 days free of charge. The signup procedure is going to be handled in a later section to ensure a smooth running from the onset.

Payment Gateways

You are here to make money. In the US and other specific countries, Amazon will pay you every two weeks through direct deposit into your preferred bank of choice. Quite simple.

For those that are overseas, the most convenient mode of payment entails signing up to the conversion option. This sees your payments converted and deposited in your bank account in the local currency. All this within just two days. Picture a broad smile on your face every 5th and 20th of every month because that will be you once you get started building your FBA business. And every subsequent payment will serve as motivation to get that deposit bigger than your previous one.

Another important consideration before going into the business is selecting your Niche. Choosing the appropriate niche is considered to be one of the most important factors for consideration. Do not dive headfirst into the products that simply seem cool enough for fast sales. It takes thorough analysis and consideration. Here are a few recommendations that should come in handy:

Category

This is more of precautionary than instructive. Amazon has a variety of categories and subcategories on the left-hand side of the lead pages. If you are new, you could have a look at the Amazon lists and get an idea of the products and the categories they fall under. On the Homepage, you can find the Search Bar that could ease the process.

Arguably, you could get any product to work on FBA as long as you can drive enough traction and traffic to it. If you are patient and determined enough to divert and build your customer base around the product then let nothing stand in your way. However, for those that wish to immediately start seeing circulation around their business, there are a couple of categories that could work best in your favor:

- Health & Personal Care
- Grocery
- Clothing & Accessories
- Beauty
- Shoes & Handbags
- Fashion & Jewelry

Time is usually of the essence. If the category is not straightforward, one of the best ways of getting the right categories is eliminating categories that do not fit your products. From there, work on finding the best fit category.

If you are classifying a product that you feel is new to the market, resist the impatient urge to categorize it under Everything Else. This is meant mainly for collectibles.

Ideas

With product success in mind, I would recommend brainstorming on a product that you could easily hone in on in one single category and pursue it to its fullest. This allows you to mainly focus on the selected niche to get the mose value out of it and truly become a master of that niche. It is vital to have a concrete plan to direct your thoughts when selecting the appropriate niche.

Best Seller Rank

Search ranking on Amazon is simply based on the number of units sold. In short, the more the one sells, the higher their rankings on Amazon. Before choosing your ideal niche, make a point of tracking your competitors' BSR's. I would recommend choosing a category that allows you to grow.

Getting started on FBA takes just 6 steps. These are meant for general guidance into a smooth start.

A.   Registration As An Amazon Seller

By now I would presume that you have already opened a Selling on Amazon account. To easily and quickly add Fulfillment by Amazon to the account, follow the following steps:

1. Go to the Amazon website and click Get Started.

2. Click on the Add FBA to your Account option.

In the event, that you do not have, yet, a Selling on Amazon account select the Register for FBA today option.

There you have it. With just these steps, you have successfully set up your FBA account and are ready to go.

B. Creating A Product Listing

This is a crucial step when getting started. Listing allows you to track factors that affect and influence your products' sales as well as the time it takes to make a sale.

1. Enter the UPC code or the ISBN code and proceed to the next screen.

2. Note the number of units available. Low numbers mean you have less competition.

3. Pay attention to the starting price. There should be a bare minimum for new products. However, if the product is used I would suggest looking for items in a similar condition to get fair pricing. You want your product to end up on the 1st or 2nd page of any related search.

4. Look at the sales rank. Understanding the sales rank takes time. For now, simply aim for low ranks as this indicates best sellers.

Listing only takes a couple of seconds. There are no upfront listing charges required until the product sells. While creating the listing your main objective should be having main keywords and great readability for the purpose of potential customers.

C. Preparing Products

This step involves packaging your products so that they could be securely and safely transported for the fulfillment cycle. The products are required to be e-Commerce ready for the Amazon Fulfillment Centers. Products that may require extra prep at the centers experience delays in reception and may also incur additional charges. Amazon also provides an FBA Prep Service if you wish for them to handle prepping your products. Per-unit fees are applicable here.

From here, you are ready to create a shipment. The following materials are recommended on hand:

- Laser or thermal printer
- Boxes
- Scale
- Measuring tape
- Product labels
- Tape
- Dunnage

- Polybags
- Bubble wrap
- Opaque Bags
- "Ready to ship" or "Sold as Set" labels.

The labels are required to be of decent quality in order to avoid fading or smearing.

D. Assigning Inventory

This step is carried out as follows:

1. In the Seller account, proceed to Inventory then Manage Inventory.

2. Select the products that you wish to be included in the FBA listings by checking the box beside them.

3. In the Actions menu, select the Change to Fulfilled by Amazon option.

4. Proceed to the next page then select Convert & Send Inventory.

When the listings are converted, in the Shipment Creation workflow, follow the outlined instructions to create the shipment to FBA.

E. Creating Shipment to FBA Centers

Here, you provide the ship-from address and show whether the shipment will be done individually or in case-packed items. From there, each item's quantity should be entered.

Beforehand, you are required to have printed the Amazon Product labels from the shipping workflow. The label should be stuck on top of the original barcode or outside any prep. This is to ensure that only Amazon Products labels are scannable.

The shipment may be split strategically to increase product availability.

F. Sending and Tracking Shipment

Before sending the shipment, the boxes or pallets ought to be labeled for proper identification purposes. Each box should have its own label. Each pallet should have four labels.

1. Once you drop the shipment off at the shipping center or the carrier picks it up, in the shipment workflow, mark it as Shipped on the Summary page.

2. In the Shipping Queue, track the shipment. In case of shipments with Shipped or In Transit status:

- Small Parcel: For updates, check the tracking numbers.

- Less than Truckload/ Full Truckload: Contact the carrier.

3. If the shipment has a Delivered status, give a 24-hour allowance before confirming the delivery location and signature receipt from the carrier.

4. When the status is Checked-In, then part of the shipment has arrived successfully at the center. Once the barcodes begin to be scanned, the status should change to Receiving.

5. Within 3-6 days the inventory should be fully received and available for sale.

The entire process does feel quite intensive. But with frequent and regular use, it gets easier. It is okay to break down the instructions for easier and personal understanding. Do not let the technicality of the process bring you down. You will easily get the hang of it with time. As I keep incessantly reiterating, a great deal of dedication is paramount in this venture.

Products

This is perhaps the most challenging part of an FBA business; buying otherwise known as sourcing. The work is not difficult but a lot of communication with manufacturers and suppliers is involved. Persistence and personal organization are vital in this process. Some challenges that may come along the way as well include a language barrier with suppliers who may be overseas.

In this chapter, we shall come across a couple of abbreviations that one is required to know and understand. They include:

- ASIN- Amazon Standard ID Number

- ISBN- International Standard Book Number

- UPC- Universal Product Code

- MSKU- Merchant Stock Keeping Unit

- FNSKU- MSKU together with ASIN

Before we handle primary sourcing from suppliers and manufacturers, let us digress a bit and look at various other ways you could purchase your products.

(i) Secondhand sourcing

This entails getting used products from yard sales, estate sales, auctions and thrift stores. You can then refurbish the products, rebrand them then list them for sale on Amazon.

(ii) Retail sourcing

This method entails getting products from retail stores, gift card sourcing, coupon engineering, salvage store sourcing and well-timed retail buys.

(iii) Bonus sourcing

This includes inventory hot lists, wholesale, Good buys through spreadsheets and hands-off sourcing.

The main objective of this chapter, however, deals with suppliers and manufacturers. The first key piece of advice I would offer is building and fostering a great relationship with your suppliers. This is not only a secret recipe for a successful FBA business but any form of business, in particular, import-export related. Quite often, competitors will spy on one another to find out each other's supplier. To come out on top of your competitors would require a strong business relationship with your supplier. For this, you ought to prove that you are reliable in matters of doing profitable business with them. How do you go about it? You may ask.

Approaching suppliers

For initial contact, this should be a professional yet personable approach. Mention something about the supplier's company or business to show prior research and be kind enough to mention what makes them stand out in your mind. Getting a referral from another company is all the better. Believe me, that personal touch to the initial contact could make the ultimate difference. It could be the stroke that struck your supplier's will to work with you. It could also make them willing to foster your business.

The process to contact the potential suppliers should proceed as follows:

(i) Build your personal list of numerous potentially good suppliers who could be reliable.

Search on the numerous search engines available to seek out potential suppliers. Background checks and reviews should help you sift out the quality ones. The LinkedIn profiles may also prove helpful when doing this check.

Contact as many suppliers as you possibly can. Ultimately you should have at least two vetted suppliers with whom you could work.

In the event, that a supplier would be unable to deliver at the given time, or fail to meet your price needs a referral could be incredibly useful.

Finally, you should have a record of all the potential suppliers that includes all their pertinent details.

(ii) Make the initial contact with the selected suppliers through a phone call or an introductory email. Either would suffice.

As I thoroughly emphasized, the initial contact should be personalized. If you obtained their contact name. Mention them personally. This shows that you are serious about doing business with them.

Just as important as the need to be personal, be specific. Go straight to the purpose of contact.

Pay attention to time differences to avoid calling your suppliers at odd hours.

Patience is key in waiting for responses from the supplier. In the event, that you have had no response from them in 5 days or so, you could make a follow-up call or email.

(iii) *Get the price quotes for the products that you desire. You can negotiate on the prices later.*

Asking for a price quote should be based on the Minimum Order Quantity. You could ask for prices breaks in the quotes are too high.

You should also inquire about the payment terms. How much up front and how much on delivery?

On negotiations, negotiate politely. Ask if you could negotiate on other costs, for instance, packaging, if the prices are fixed.

A Couple of Pointers For Negotiating:

- Do not negotiate too soon. First, establish that you are creating a huge brand and seeking a long-term business relationship. Speaking long term eases your position in the negotiations.

- Communicate that you wish to start small. An initial order for a couple of units, perhaps in the lower hundreds to observe the market response. However, volumes would increase as the brand grows.

- Ensure that you are speaking to the right person to obtain good prices.

(iv) Request samples of the products that you wish to order. Pictures would not be enough to tell the quality of a product. Seeing and touching them physically is the bar to determining a product's quality.

If it so happens that the quality of the product is satisfactory you could then make your initial order.

As you wait for your samples to arrive, you can go ahead and order your competitor's products from Amazon. This allows you to compare the quality of your products and theirs once the samples arrive.

Edging Past Your Competition

The strategy in this business is to be able to sell your items for a premium price. In order to do this, you have to make your products better than what your competitors are offering. To gain this advantage, view the Amazon reviews on your main competitors. Look particularly for the negative reviews. This helps you figure out what the customers dislike about a certain product.

From here, you can talk to the supplier to make the necessary modifications to cater to the needs of the customers. Most suppliers will be more than willing to do so as long as the business terms are well agreed on. The cost per unit may increase but then a higher selling price will balance the books. And the good news of all this: your product becomes the premium high-quality product in your respective niche.

You could also buy your competitors' products to understand how they specifically promote the product. This could actually include joining their program and studying the emails they send you since emails could be a part of their promotional means. If the brand is a successful one, all you need to do is set up a similar method and tweak it to suit your own product.

Lastly, you could also buy the poorly rated products. Doing a contrast with your product ensures that you do not go wrong when it comes to quality.

When looking for suppliers, Alibaba is going to be your best friend in terms of business to business space. Take time to pick out the most suitable supplier according to your preference. There are other companies that could also come in handy when looking for suppliers:

- http://www.ttnet.net/
- http://www.hktdc.com/en-buyer/
- http://www.oempromo.com/
- http://www.made-in-china.com/
- http://www.hellotrade.com/
- http://www.indiamart.com/
- http://www.globalsources.com/
- http://www.manufacturers.com.tw/

- http://www.thomasnet.com/

If you are looking for suppliers from search engines, try to perform advanced searches. You can also include key search phrases to trim and reduce the number of irrelevant results.

Dealing with Suppliers

The following are the best practices when dealing with your suppliers. They will make you come off as a professional as well as making your relationship more effective and practically easier.

1. Always have a backup to your supplier, no matter how ideal the current one is. The backup should stand in when something arises with your initial supplier ensuring that our customers will not be cut off.

2. Visit your supplier's location if possible. This boosts your credibility to the supplier as a genuine person and business.

3. Do the due diligence necessary. If you want a solid supplier and solid clients for that matter, you had better own your part as well.

4. Be professional and confident and the rest falls into place.

Branding and Packaging

You do not want your product to be just like any other out there in the market. Here, we shall look at how to make your product stand out from the rest. This is how to position your products to be premium in the market. You not only sell the product at a premium but also get your customers to have a great experience therein.

The biggest question you should ask yourself here is: Who is my customer? Before starting this process, you should know and understand your target audience well. This determines the packaging look of the product as well as the incentives to offer once the customers make purchases.

For this purpose, your appeal will cut across:

- Customers who wish to purchase long lasting premium products.

- Customers who are looking for the IT factor in their items of purchase.

- Customers who want more than an ordinary feeling for their items of purchase. Those that want to feel a certain type of way with the product.

It could be argued that consumers are out there to save money, thus it makes more financial sense to sell cheaper products. However, it is worth noting that consumers are always willing to pay more to get a great product and that feeling of innate satisfaction. This means that most purchases will have an associated element of emotion to them. This is where you come in with a premium product assured of a loyal following that will keep coming back for your product.

The packaging, just as the product, has to bring out that premium status element. This means working on the packaging's visual appeal to reflect the premium status. First impression count. Great and eye-catching packaging creates a perceived value that allows you to sell at a higher price. In fact, you could sell fewer units than your competitors but still, make decent profits from the higher margins.

If you're among the few with a knack for design, you can come up with your own packaging. If not, you can easily commission professional graphic artists to create the package design. Some reliable sites to find artists include:

- 99designs.com
- Upwork.com
- Freelancer.com

In fact, you could start off with a cheap but decent design. Once the profits start growing, you can hire professionals to get that premium packaging design. For good design, you should be looking out for:

- Crisp, clear and clean text, lines and images.
- Simple design.

- High resolution on the text and images.

- A strong and stand-out statement.

I would recommend sending a packaging insert in every package purchased. This is what excellent customer service is all about. It shows that you are available and ready to offer them support.

Product Names

This is where you require some classic brainstorming to come up with the right name for your product. You should come up with a name that is suitable for your niche and market. Catchy names always do the trick. The trick is ever to resonate with your potential target audience. In order to have a rough idea of how to generate ideas, you can look through your competitor's brand or product names.

For the website addresses, always opt for the .com URL. If the address is not available, you may add a relevant word such as product, company to increase the viability. Back to the product names, when listing on Amazon, search optimization should work in your favor. This means using keywords that are clear for your potential clients. Nice and compact titles with just a couple of strong keywords.

With all these in mind, I believe you are more than adequately prepared to deliver premium products to your potential client base. As seen, getting to premium status does require a lot of input from you as the seller. From constant and persistent communication with your suppliers to catchy brand names and packaging. This is not meant to be easy, otherwise, the margins would not be as lucrative as they are. This journey is only treacherous in the beginning. Once the Amazon deposits start raking in, all the blood and sweat is going to be worth every drop.

Listing

At this point, you have already ordered the product. The next step is to ensure that the product listing stands out from the rest on Amazon. The goal here is to come up with a product list that has a high conversion rate. When you create a top-notch product list not only will you stand out from your current competitors but you will also stand apart from future competitors. When listing your product, you will need to be keen on the factors that affect your sales as well as the duration it takes to make the sales.

Unlike other e-Commerce platforms, listing on Amazon is fairly simple and fast. It could even take just a couple of seconds. More so, there are no fees paid upfront for listing. Payments are only made once your product is purchased. Since payments are made to Amazon, no items sold go unpaid. The process is also less cumbersome since you do not have to work yourself out getting images for your products. Furthermore, you still do need any templates. This, in turn, saves you a lot of time to focus on sourcing and selling your product.

Amazon listing is one of the most important things you will do in this business. In the listing, there are a couple of important aspects that ought to be considered:

Product Title

Back in the days, the trick used by sellers was to use plenty of main keywords for the product titles. However, Amazon caught up with this trend and tweaked things all across the entire board. Amazon now has a character limit on all the product titles. All new sellers are required to comply with the new rule. The older ones could remain unchanged but on the strict condition that they remain unaltered.

The key to reaping optimally from the product title revolves around two major factors: Having concise main keywords and great readability for the potential customers. This means coming up with specific and eye-catching keywords that would easily draw the attention of potential clients.

Conversion Rate

Conversion rate essentially means the percentage of customers who purchase a product over the entire number of customers who visit the product page or site. A good number of e-Commerce outlets average a measly 1-2%. Yes, just 1 or 2 people out of a 100 visiting the site make an actual purchase. Now with FBA, things could take an interesting twist. All factors considered, you could average at least a 10% conversion rate. That figure sounds astronomical, does it not? Well, I personally average around 13-25% every day on my personal products. How so?

- Choosing the right niche

- Finding trustworthy suppliers

- Creating solid product listings

When you give as much, if not more, input and a bit of patience to this business you are bound to be part of the success story if not the poster boy.

In order to be leaps ahead in your listings, we need to understand how the actual process works. Listing is driven by Amazon's Search Engine Optimization. The Amazon Search Engine Optimization algorithm consists of the following factors:

(i) ***A high rate of conversion***- The percentage of clients who purchase a product after visiting the page.

(ii) ***A high rate of click-through***- The percentage of customers who click on your product list after viewing it from a search.

(iii) ***High sales velocity***- The number of products sold in a specific period of time.

(iv) ***Reviews***- The number of positive product reviews.

These factors are important because they bring into focus products that have high conversion and click-through rates. This shows customers' preferences for your listing over others with the willingness to purchase your products more often than your competitors. The more sales you make, the better the conversion and click-through rates. This means Amazon is making more money. Your product quickly scales up to the first page of the search results. More views, yet more sales! In fact, you could become so successful that Amazon advertises on your behalf. If your listing does convert well, then why not help you to sell more products?

Creating an Amazon Listing

If you already have a Seller Account, proceed to Inventory then click on Add a Product. This option assumes that you are selling a product that already exists on Amazon. Thus, the process is quite easy to navigate.

It is worth noting that some categories on Amazon are restricted. This means you have to manually apply for approval to sell in the categories. These include:

- Beauty
- Jewelry
- Clothing & Accessories
- Luggage & Travel Accessories
- Health & Personal Accessories
- Shoes, Handbags & Sunglasses

However, we shall have a look at how to build your own brand. Click on Create a New Product. From here search a category that fits your product. I presume the prior research had given the necessary information on choosing the categories. Do not fret over this, nonetheless, a different category may be assigned to your product later.

Each category comes with its own requirements. But all it takes is proof of conforming to all the requirements to simply get approval. The best thing about approval is the fact it blocks out a huge chunk of casual sellers from your respective niche. In this respect, you should try to avoid having your first product in the kitchen mold. In my opinion, this is among the lowest barrier entry categories.

For you to be ready to put your products on sale, you would only be required to fill in the starred boxes:

(I) Product Name- the title that potential customers will see. It should be short but descriptive. This is because the name appears on your FNSKU.

This also becomes part of the URL to your Amazon Listing.

(Ii) Brand Name.

(Iii) Manufacturer- normally similar to your brand.

(Iv) EAN Or UPC.

Let's have a look at UPC.

UPC Code

You are required to have for all the product listings. The UPC code is a series of numbers that an individual retailer inputs to their system. These codes are simply bought online for just a couple of dollars. A minimum of 10 codes should go for around $20.

After adding the UPC code, Amazon creates their internal FNSKU from the code then assign it to your products.

Price

Moving forward, select the Offer tab and enter the condition of the product as New and then add the price.

What is the ideal pricing? The trick here is to look at the average price of your competitors and add a few dollars on top. The price can always be changed later. A common marketing ploy is inflating the initial price then fixing the sale price where you actually wish to sell it. This makes the product look like it is on a sale.

Back to the listing, scroll down to ensure that the shipping method reads FBA.

Retrieving the FNSKU

In essence, the FNSKU is all that you may require at this juncture. And you might be wondering why this is even significant to your shipping. Well, as it turns out, you will need to receive this to enable you to complete the packaging of your wares. It is a requirement for all good in the warehouses of Amazon. This then goes to say that you will be subjected to an extra cost so that you may be able to print a new FNSKU label that will be placed over that of the already existent UPC code. But it is not all gloom. The up side to the whole situation is that you have the liberty to jump over that step and directly print the FNSKU as part of the packaging of your goods.

However, there are some things you must take note of if you are to take this route. You need to be aware that choosing this path then will consequently limit you to only making sales of your goods through fulfillment by Amazon. In the event, that you decide that you want to expand the operations from just FBA and explore other options available to your e-commerce business, then it would require you to print again your UPC code with the image that would have alternatively been purchased from a website service dealing in the sale of UPC codes.

For the retrieving of the FNSKU, go to the inventory tab and click on it, click on the manage inventory button and from here, choose "Print Item Labels" that will appear in a drop-down option coming in next to the product option. There are various formats that one can choose from. However, the 1" * 2-5/8", 30-Up labels is a popular choice.

Shipping

This could arguably be one of the most technical parts. Here the learning curve gets a little steep. Each shipping company and supplier is different from the next. However, on subscribing to one of the Amazon programs, you would only be required to learn just a fraction of what goes on out there. Amazon does most of the heavy lifting for you.

The entire process boils down to:

1. Your supplier packages your product and the boxes get shipped to the port.

2. The cargo is then loaded on a sea vessel or an aircraft.

3. Sea shipments are unloaded, pass through customs and then shipped to your preferred mailing service such as FedEx. Air shipments go directly to Amazon but may pass through customs under some certain conditions.

4. Once the shipment arrives at the Amazon warehouses then processed, your product is ready for launch.

This is assuming your product is being manufactured internationally (which is often the case). The steps will be simpler if the product is manufactured domestically.

Freight Forwarders

These are companies that you can hire to represent you and handle all of your shipping needs. They will be the customs broker. They should also temporarily hold your shipment in a warehouse. Here they can relabel the shipment boxes then send them off to Amazon centers.

Whichever company that you choose, you have to do some vetting and paperwork to make sure they're the right fit for you at the right price point. You will also be in close contact with them. This includes numerous faxes, phone calls and emails. This should put you in the position of controlling your business as well as keeping records.

Traction and Feedback

After learning the basics of shipping and you have had your first sales, there are some things need to be taken into consideration as they are essential in our business. The traction of your business refers to the progress that your firm, especially a start-up business and the progress it is making as it grows; is the speed slow or fast or is the pace at which it develops as expected?

In business, it is often difficult to get your business to kick off running and selling which in turn brings you profits and raises you the cash you require to either repay debts and clear with the bank or start finding new ways of improving the business. The resources that are needed to get your FBA business off and to run might not be available, or you are short a few coins, but your reputation might be at stake if you do not keep above the curve of the business and the competition as well.

In this chapter, I am going to take you through what traction is like when you are beginning to sell on FBA and the type of feedback that will work for you and how to manage it.

A) *Traction*

For businesses to measure their success, customer response and the revenues that they make ultimately tell a company how well they are doing compared to the competition and market. There is no real way to measure traction, but these two are ways that can help a business keep track of how well they are faring.

Traction in business is important for many reasons, but the main one is for investors. Each business has certain investors who have a particular interest in the company they are inputting money. The traction that a company makes is what attracts other investors into the business. This influx of more investors also is the way to increase funds that will be at the disposal of the business to help it improve.

Therefore, the same notion is applied to an FBA business. As an entrepreneur, this is your business and the amount of traction that you will make in the first couple of months, weeks, days, all depends on how you want to the business to progress—this will determine whether you will get more investors into your business or not.

The investors might be your parents, friends or yourself. It can be a way to know if this is a venture you can proceed with or if you should try something else. It is important for you to create traction for your FBA business, as it is part of your business growth plan.

Traction, though it cannot be measured, can help steer the business I the right direction of enough effort by the entrepreneur is put injected into the business.

The feedback that you get from customers will help you

- Make changes in the way the company runs

- Add or remove some of the processes that you are currently using

- Adopt a new strategy suggested by your customers

- Create a good relationship with your customers

Traction can be measured through:
Sales you are making

- The response from customers

- The market research you have done after starting your business

These can be some of the ways as it all depends on the way that you have set your metrics that will determine the success of your business. But in FBA, traction is measured through customer's response or feedback that you get from your clients.

It is okay if you struggle with traction since you are new in the business. Many startups fail because of lack of knowledge of the product they are currently selling; that is:

- The awareness of the product

- The competition

- The market niche

To make you different from the other new FBA users, ensure that you have done your due diligence and really understand the space you're working in. Make sure that you have:

- Researched on how to run your startup, as a beginner in FBA Amazon, you are running a startup business.

- Reached out to customers beforehand to know what they want and cannot get, that you can provide.

This will set you apart. The likelihood of you failing is minimal due to the market research you have done in advance. Customers can make or break a business when they are not involved in your plans.

Research all things pertaining FBA Amazon; such its pricing strategies, the fees and the ranks of sale as well as how to keep an inventory of your stock—all these things can go a long way to help you be better than your competitors, even those who have been in the business for a long time.

B) Feedback

Once you have established yourself as a seller on FBA, and have sold some of your products you want to focus on increasing sales and growing your business. One of the best strategies for accomplishing this is by getting feedback about your products and services.

Establishing a feedback section on your site or product is important. You can create a feedback section on your orders; though most people doubt this is possible when you are a beginner.

You can qualify for feedback as a seller even though Amazon.com is handling fulfillment procedures. There are three ways - and plenty more- that can help you to acquire feedback on your orders while on FBA.

We will look at three tips:

1. Take into consideration FBA specific campaigns

Creating awareness about your store to potential clients is key. It is best to create an email or message attached to your product, after purchase that explains your role in the Amazon fulfillment model and ask them to confirm that everything went as expected. Let them know that you want to hear their feedback and that you can help make things right if they are dissatisfied.

To test this, craft the message that you want to be used and send it at different times with the notion that a buyer has a 90-day window to leave feedback once they have placed an order.

There are those entrepreneurs who will estimate the time when the product will arrive at the customer's' destination and send the message then or as close as possible to that day. Others will provide the client with a few days to get the product and determine if it is as they expected or if they are dissatisfied with the product.

To build FBA- specific solicitation campaigns, together with your timing and message, some sellers offer a 14-day free trial period. This will help you build your own solicitation rules based on the delivery date. Ensure that you follow the rules that are placed when creating your solicitations.

2. Confirm That You Are Soliciting

As I stated before, most beginners in the FBA arena always presume that they are not allowed to have or get feedback on their orders, their FBA- fulfilled orders. Amazon states that customers are allowed to leave comments on the orders that have been transacted by Amazon, for sellers to view. This is the same for merchant-fulfilled orders.

The FBA orders can work wonders for you as an entrepreneur. The sales can hit the roof and also this can be a way for you to increase your reputation as a seller, even though you are new in the market.

Things you would want feedback from your customers on:

- Communication with the seller
- The packaging of the product(s)
- Shipping process
- Customer service

- Dispute resolution- which has to be on point.

Amazon usually, if not always, helps an average seller to have the best shipping and packaging services that puts them on equal footing with professional dealers.

3. Be Extra Careful On What You Are "Acquiring"

With FBA orders, the same as any other orders run through or by Amazon; when customers are not satisfied with the product they purchased or with any of the fulfillment services that are provided by Amazon, the feedback received, Amazon will strike through.

If anything does go wrong, there is a chance that the problem mainly isn't with you but with Amazon. The FBA solicitation process value increases so does the tracking changes that your feedback score provides.

You have the option of tracking your comments manually. You need to do this as often as you possibly can. To do this;

- Bookmark the Amazon Feedback Manager section in your Seller Central dashboards.

Ratings daily may vary considerably all dependent on the volume of your orders. The more orders you get, the number of ratings will increase as well.

You could also use FeedbackFive that is an automatic way of looking at your feedback. How this works is there will be alerts that will notify you of negative, neutral or new feedback.

You can receive the comment in either mail or text form. This is less stressful for you; since you don't have to spend hours going through your dashboard to see if there is any new feedback.

To clear any disputes with your customer that have resulted from your errors, make sure you resolve the issue as fast as you can by taking the necessary steps to do so. After you've done everything you can to fix the issue, then and only then, can you ask for a removal of the negative feedback. In case you believe it is Amazon's fault, you can request for them to remove the negative feedback.

In point form:

- The FBA orders can help you garner positive feedback for your business

- Create the message you want to use for your customers

- Solicit as soon as possible today if you can

- Test various timing rules

- Strategize ways of keeping track of your results

All these will play a significant role in your business and increase your reputation as a seller, immensely.

E-Commerce Redefined

Tricks and Tactics

It is easy to get swayed and mixed up with a lot of unnecessary things, or at least things that aren't important in the moment, that you feel will help you succeed. However, narrowing your focus and taking it one step at a time will help you focus on what matters. We took the liberty to create a list of tips and tricks that will be in line with this and help you achieve your goals.

1. How To Deal With Negative Reviews.

The world is becoming increasingly smaller with the advancement of the internet. One person can reach millions in a matter of minutes. Why is this relevant regarding bad reviews? Well, this is because customers are the best marketing strategy you can employ. This is rather ambiguous, and by customers, we mean anyone who has consumed your product—not just exclusively people who are happy with it. Dissatisfied customers may leave bad reviews which are terrible for your business. This is because potential clients will often look at reviews before they decide whether or not to buy your product. Therefore, a bad review could dent your business and its reputation.

In general, offering excellent customer service is a good solution. Nonetheless, most clients will still feel the need to express their displeasure the moment something goes wrong.

You can comment on the review and express your apologies for the issue at hand, you can contact the customer and try to make things right. But most of the time, the best way to handle it is by getting as many other positive reviews as you can. Positive reviews will dilute the negative reviews and reduce their effect on your sales.

Another thought to note is that Amazon typically removes negative reviews if the complaint was due to their error and not the seller's. This is to help protect the seller and keep their sales from suffering if Amazon fails to hold up their end of the transaction.

These next tricks are for on how you can save money:

2. Free Inventory From Your House

In my house, and I'm damn sure your house as well, there are those items that you have not used, ever! not since you bought it because it was on sale, or there was a discount on the commodity. You could have used it once and return to the furthest corner of your closet or kitchen cabinet; no matter the case, these items can be turned into cash or better, profit! All you have to do is ship them to Amazon for that to happen.

Go hunting! Look through your bookshelves, not all books in your library you like them, get them out and create space for the series you have been dying to read in your house and also reduce clutter. Go into your cabinets in your kitchen, your kids (if you have any) rooms with their permission, of course, your room as well and get rid of anything that you do not use at all. Some items you can get will surprise you; as these items can be used to create profits on Amazon.

Take the initiative and involve your family, friends, and neighbor-if they are willing to do so-and use all these items to earn cash! It can be an excellent way to spend a weekend, go through your trash to make money.

3. Joining Amazon FBA Facebook Groups

The easiest and cheapest way to garner tons of information is by joining the Amazon FBA community on Facebook, or FB. They always have content that will help you in making more profits and also manage your business better than you are.

Scrounge through the archived posts on the community site and also ask questions, you are guaranteed an answer. These forums are a way for you to learn more about the business which issues affect most start-up businesses on Amazon FBA and get to know which tricks you can use to make things easier for you.

There is a full-time FBA Facebook group recommended for you to join and other groups as well on Facebook. Do your research beforehand then go on Fb and find the best group for you to join.

4. Using Dunnage For Shipments

The stuff, either puffy or protective wrapper, which you use to wrap your load to protect them from touching the sides of your shipping box that is the definition of dunnage.

There are various things you can use to protect your items so that they can arrive safely to your customer without breakage. The commodities in the list below are things you are most likely going to have in your house already. You can use:

- A newspaper blanket

- A variety of small cardboard boxes for glass items

- Tie printed papers in your everyday plastic grocery bags. This is to protect your shipment from getting in contact with the newsprint.

5. Free Boxes From Grocery Stores For Shipment

At the beginning of your Amazon FBA business, there won't be the need for you to pay for delivery boxes as you might not have the cash for it or you want to save the money you have for something else. You can get shipping boxes for free from grocery stores, your neighbors who have moved recently, or your friends or colleagues that have moved as well as places that recycle their old boxes. This will save you tons of cash. Make sure you select the best boxes out of all those that are at your disposal.

From the grocery store, ask the employees or attendees when they are restocking their shelves if you can have some of the boxes they are using. They are likely to let you come and collect to your heart's content or even when they are restocking come and get the boxes from their aisles.

6. Lighter Fluid To Remove Price Stickers

When reusing shipment boxes, there is the likelihood of price stickers being on them. Removing them is one struggle you will have to endure if you are trying to save money, but getting rid of the sticker residue is another struggle all on its own.

I do recommend using Goo Gone when dealing with residue from price stickers. There is an easier alternative to you going to the shop and getting yourself a bottle of Goo Gone, use lighter fluid.

Be careful when handling the liquid, and this will guarantee removal of the residue. The process is quite simple, and all you will require is a Scotty peeler to remove the labels. You can use a Ronsonol lighter fluid. To do this, you will:

- Pour some of the lighter fluid on the sticker residue you want to get rid off

- Wait for a few minutes, approximately 5 minutes before you can try and remove the labels

- Using your Scotty peeler, gently try and pry the tag off.

You will realize that with the lighter fluid compared to the Goo Gone, it will come right off and won't be sticky at all! While the Goo Gone will take you a couple of tries to remove the label off and it still is sticky.

There is a slippery oily residue left behind by the Goo Gone, you will get it off, but the label will come right off. To get rid of the stickiness of the bottle or box, use a paper towel and apply some liquid fluid to it and rub on the sticky are, it will be no more!

7. Free Inventory From Freecycle.Org

Join a group of your area on Freecycle Network to be able to see what people are getting rid of or giving away for free that you can use for your shipments. You might be shocked by the number of things that you can source using this network. I got board games- both used and new-; books, in boxes; kitchen appliances, among other things.

The way it works is:

- Claim an item on the Freecycle Network

- The owner will leave it on the front porch or sidewalk

- Go and collect your item!

And that's it! Fairly easy and straightforward. This makes it easy for you to coordinate with the owner as you will get to set a time that you will pass by to collect it. Much more comfortable than how Craigslist works.

Do not go alone when doing your pick-ups! We don't want a case of people disappearing or it being a horror movie straight out of a Stephen King novel. Take care as you don't know who you are going to collect your item from. Safety first, the commodity can wait a day or two before you go and receive it.

8. Boxes From Arbitrage Purchases

To be honest, most of the sourcing that we do for this type of business is through online sourcing. This means that there will be shipments sent to you in boxes. Thus, you can use these same boxes for your shipments to Amazon. But you have to be careful and remove all barcodes. This can be removed or covered up before you can use the UPS label or Amazon.

There are times when you just need to have a nap without worrying over unnecessarily about the way your online store is doing or how the shipments are faring or remember if you sent a reply to your customer's comment.

Below are some productivity tools that can help you shave off some of that time:

IFTTT (If This Then That)- this is mainly used by sellers on Amazon or eBay. The app is used to alert the sellers of when sales have been made, or stock has been added back into inventory, or it has been added elsewhere. The purpose of this app can be used for various reasons such as:

- To buy a used book for less than a dollar

- You can make your recipes of IFTTT like implement price drop alerts

Facebook News Eradicator - with various sellers mainly spending their time on this social media platform going through the different FBA groups, it can take much of your time without you realizing it.

To help you with this, this eradicator cuts down your extension extremely low. It allows you not to spend so much time on the internet getting to know what all your sources on Amazon FBA are talking about or all seller community groups.

Cleer Pro- is an online app for online arbitrage. It is a software that makes it easier for you as a vendor to browse easily when trying to look for deals, items or doing your research on Amazon.com

The software is for free! Go and make the most of it.

Gmail Canned Responses- typing a similar response over and over again can get exhausting, and no one wants that kind of stress. Therefore, this app allows you to formulate a response that is going to reply automatically to the type of replies that come from your customers. The same app can be used to respond to an email you get in your Amazon seller inbox. Since Amazon allows you to use your email to respond to customers instead of creating a particular kind of email address, you can use this app.

The only downside is that you cannot use Yahoo or Outlook for this, it only works if you have a Gmail account. The best way to use this is to avoid having your responses including website addresses that aren't your own Amazon web site.

Flashback Express - it can only be used on Windows, unfortunately. It can be used to quickly capture and annotate your voice and then upload the video to your screen. This can be used to communicate something that is in your store. Or deliver something that is on your screen to a colleague or your occasional customer.

This makes the message more personal than ever, and it can be the best way to explain something to your customers in an easier manner, and it can make you quite popular with other clients. It can bring you more customers as well.

- What is required from you:

- Download the app

- Get a built-in microphone (if you already have one, the better) or get a peripheral microphone

- Attach to it and get cracking!

Unroll.me - there are dozens upon dozens of emails that you receive from a seller on a daily basis about different offers that you are going to get from Amazon. The difference between having this app and not having it, is you are required to need to keep clicking delete or unsubscribe manually.

This app allows you to unsubscribe from those emails or offers that you do not want to have in bulk. There are tutorials online that you can use to help you navigate through the app with ease.

Other hacks that can help alleviate your work as a seller on Amazon FBA include:

> 1. To save your time as a salesperson when screening your items and scanning them, you can use the $0.00 buy cost to help you when browsing for items mainly in the app's field "Buy$."

The time that you spend typing at the expense of the item is deducted since it costs nothing! You can use a calculator to subtract the actual buying price of the item from the profit price and decide on whether you will purchase the item or you will forgo it.

At times, it is not necessary for you to do the math of whether you will get to buy the product; all you have got to do is check if the price you are buying the item is higher or lower than the price of the profit you are bound to make.

An example would be if the cost of the headgear is at $12.99 and the profit you are required to make is at $9.99; you will not buy the item since it costs more than what you are going to get from the profit.

> 2. Other ways of reducing the scanning process are through downloading the Amazon

1Button app. It is an extension from chrome that shows you the price of the item you require, and it does the searching or looking or scanning for you.

An instance would be when looking for game boards; the app will let you know if the game is sold on Amazon and the price of the game. This saves you the trouble of going through Amazon trying to find the game and if it is even available and the price as well.

Keep in mind that not always does the search engine provide the results that you are looking for and at times the items might not even be available or found.

- Make sure you invest in the best supplies you possibly can get your hands on. There are the common denominators of supplies that most Amazon sellers have in their arsenal and use them. Most of them swear by these items and can attest to their immense help when carrying out their daily sales.

For example, as I explained before, removing price stickers can be an absolute mess, and the struggle is real, we can all attest to that. Therefore, the time spent trying to pry the stickers off with your fingernails, hurting yourself in the process and using about 10 minutes to take one out when you have a hoard of them; you can use Goo Gone and a Scotty Peeler. As a fellow Amazon seller, make sure that you invest fully in these commodities to ease your struggles while doing the job.

- These items are a must have:

- Goo Gone

- Scotty Peeler

- Shipping tape that has a tape dispenser - I'm sure previously you weren't using a shipping tape but your standard packaging tape, which won't work. The distance covered is different, to say the least, and it must have been torturous trying to pack your items. The tape is bound to stick to the tape roll and getting the edge of the tape must be a struggle on its own.

3. Have a business credit card and checking account- in your daily life, you have a personal credit card that you use mainly to buy your items and spend it as you wish. You also, most definitely (if not, get one ASAP!) keep track of your expenses and savings as well.

You can have a software tracking app on your every expense charged to your credit card, be it personal or business. For the Amazon FBA, you need to have a business credit card and checking account to keep track of what you are spending on and where your money goes. This card and account need to be different from your credit and checking account.

You can use Quickbooks as a way to keep track of your personal and business accounts and credit cards. The app allows you to:

- Keep track of what you have spent

- Know how much you owe your credit card and

- Where you shop at

4. With this being your business, even if you are running it at your house, you need to run it like one. To make shipping easier, create your shipping and prepping station.

It doesn't have to be anything fancy or too elaborate, get a small table and lean it against a wall. Have drawers (they could be colored or whatever pattern you prefer) close by that house all your poly bags, shipping tapes, scissors, liquid fluid and any other necessary appliance that you need to wrap your shipping items and put them in your box.

Having or creating order in your house can help you run your business very smoothly. The station will help you reduce the time spent running around looking for scissors, the shipping tape or trying to figure out where to lay your merchandise at so that you can work.

The area around your working station can function as your prepping station, where you gather all your necessary items, put them together before you move to your working station to put the final touches on your product before shipping them off to your customer.

The station can act as a studio of some sort. When you have laid out your items on the table, you can take a picture of the items and use them for your store on Amazon. The pictures can be edited; changing the color in the background to pure white t put it on your product listing images section of your site.

5. It has become a thousand times easier to print out your Amazon FBA bar-code or better known as FNSKU and your shipping labels direct to the thermal printer that you own (if you don't have it, you can purchase one from Seller Central). The labels are created using AZLabels.

How to get it to work to print your barcodes:

- Download the AZLabels extension from their Chrome extension, and it works on Mac and PC systems. The instructions on how to create an account with them are included after you download the extension.

- Once you have created an account, you get to list and create your shipping plan as normal as you possibly can.

- When you get to the part of printing your labels for your Amazon bar-code, there is a Print Thermal Labels button; press it to get your printed label from your DYMO 450 Turbo printer or any other printer that you own.

- There is a PDF file that you are provided with to check out your labels. You get to change the size of the labels as well as the margins then you are ready to print out your labels. You get your printed labels in plenty.

Now on how to print Amazon shipping labels:

- The same process you used to print out your bar codes is used to print your Amazon shipping labels.

- Until you get to the section where you are ready to print your shipping tags, then you get to pick between Print box labels and Print Thermal Labels. Not many people use the feature, though some people use laser printers, you can use thermal printers as well.

All these methods provided to you are to aid you in ensuring that when you handle your Amazon FBA account as flawlessly as it is possible.

Conclusion

Amazon offers two ways for you to sell your products on their website. One involves handling everything yourself, including customer service, shipments, and almost every detail of the process. The other method involves having them handle everything from shipping to customer service to refunds and exchanges, and more. The second method is referred to as Fulfillment by Amazon, often abbreviated to simply FBA. There are many perks to both methods, but Fulfillment by Amazon is tailor-made for those people that aren't simply selling a few items, don't own a warehouse, cannot or don't wish to hire a staff, don't want to constantly work on shipping out hundreds of small packages, and don't want the added headache of handling customer service. The added benefits of having Amazon (via Fulfillment by Amazon) handle a bulk of the work includes offering customers every possible perk available, such as free two-day shipping for Prime members, quality assurance, and excellent customer service from a provider that can be trusted.

While the path of selling in large quantities online is not always an easy one, it is a rewarding path to take. Not only is it a business where there's no true boss (unless you hire someone), but it is extremely scalable, doesn't require a lot of special skills, and doesn't involve the extremely steep startup costs that typical brick and mortar or dedicated retail website businesses incur. While it does require capital to purchase products, it doesn't require heavy marketing up front (more on this later), and it doesn't require you to be an expert salesperson. One of the best perks is that you can truly dip your toes in a bit before going into it fulltime. It can be handled as a second income stream that will grow and blossom into a main source of income. It can truly become your escape from the nine to five grind from there if you are dedicated to that goal.

The process is not painfully difficult, and once a seller gets the swing of things, the only issue limiting the potential profits is a willingness to work hard and ability to be persistent. While the process itself is easy, you should not mistake this as easy money. This is not a get-rich-quick method, and if you're a serial entrepreneur you've probably learned that none of the promises involved with such schemes tend to pan out. While Amazon will fulfill the orders and handle the shipment and customer service, that doesn't mean you can afford to simply sit around. Quite the opposite is true. Instead, your time is freed up to continuously be on the lookout for new products that are worth selling, building your business, and for some, even time to create your own products and brands. This is how a one-person retail operation is possible: Amazon does a large number of the menial tasks for you so you can focus on finding the profitable products.

The journey can be a slow one, or it can be a fast one. It is entirely dependent on how much work, time, and energy is expended by the seller. The great thing is that almost ANYONE can be successful at it, and with a little bit of insider knowledge, you should have no problem getting started and learning the ropes. Taking your time to do some research now, you're setting yourself up to avoid some of the most obvious mistakes made by even the most successful FBA sellers in the business when they first started, and for that, I commend you greatly. Are you ready to get started?

www.ingramcontent.com/pod-product-compliance
Lightning Source LLC
Chambersburg PA
CBHW031424210526
45464CB00005B/2033